Lots of
LANGUAGES

Phrasebook & Reference Guide

For Teachers, Tutors, ESL, and Language Learners

Susan A. Worline, M. Ed

Edited by Michael Yoon Chen

INF■NI
P R E S S

New York, New York

Library of Congress Control Number 2006921878
ISBN 1-932457-05-4

Infini Press LLC
info@infinipress.com
www.infinipress.com

Printed in the United States of America

TABLE OF CONTENTS

AUTHOR'S NOTE

I compiled this phrasebook out of desperation. After a lot of frustration and expense purchasing several language dictionaries, books, workbooks and CDs for preparation as an ESL teacher, I wanted to find less cumbersome and more concise resources. Since there were none, I decided to develop a phrasebook that could be used by everybody, but especially by ESL teachers, content-area teachers, tutors, ESL students and exchange students. Language learners may find it useful as well as people who travel around the world on business. This phrasebook is my contribution to one-stop global language shopping.

Susan A. Worline, M.ED

EDITOR'S NOTE

We have edited this book with English-speaking educators in mind and chose to romanize all non-roman languages. We at times have had heated discussions on which way to present the translation. When there were many ways to say the same thing, we chose the phrase most suited to the classroom. The intention was to make it easier for English-speaking teachers to be able to communicate with non-English-speaking students. The priority was given to sounds of the language over the accurate accent marks for tones, especially for languages such as Vietnamese.

We sincerely hope that this reference book helps you communicate with new students who do not know much English. We always welcome your comments and feedback.

Michael Yoon Chen

ACKNOWLEDGEMENT

Many thanks and my gratitude to the Hilliard Davidson and Hilliard Darby High School ESL (English as a Second Language) students for their good humor and help in creating this book. Without their help, this phrasebook would not have been completed.

Also, many thanks and appreciation to my colleagues and dedicated ESL teachers Becky Sanders and Nikki Monroe for their support as well as the administration of the Hilliard City School District.

Editorial staff also thank additional translators and educational consultants.

Arabic	Eman Mohammad, Osman Muhidin
Brazilian Portuguese	Fabrícia Duell
Chinese-Mandarin	Frederick Chen, Wayne Huang
Farsi	Maryam Hallez, Sheyda and Manshid Ferdosian
French	François Le Roy
Gujarati	Naseem Alibhai, Kurangi Patel
Hindi	Naseem Alibhai, Ajay Verma, Niketa Patel
Hmong	Yee Yang
Japanese	Akiko Sawada, Kaneto Fukuhara
Korean	Michael Nahm, Yoonyoung Lee
Russian	Slava Kroutikov
Somali	Mohamud Farah
Swahili	Bazi Ahmed
Vietnamese	Chuong Dao, Phuong Chung, Dan Trinh

Arabic

Arabic is considered sacred since it is the formal written language of the Koran (Qur'an), the holy book of Islam. Arabic is also the oral liturgical language of the Arab world and widely studied among Muslims throughout the world. Arabic is the most widespread of the Semitic languages, spoken in Algeria, Bahrain, Comoros, Chad, Djibouti, Egypt, Iraq, Jordan, Kuwait, Lebanon, Libya, Mauritania, Morocco, Oman, Qatar, Saudi Arabia, Somalia, Sudan, Syria, Tunisia, United Arab Emirates, Palestine (West Bank and Gaza), Western Sahara (SADR), and Yemen. It is also a national language of Mali and Senegal (Hassaniya).

Arabic is written and read from right to left. The Arabic alphabet has 28 letters.

Arabic letters

a	pronounced as 'a' is tag.
u	pronunciation close to the letter 'i'.
i	pronounced as 'i' in kit.
â	pronunced as a long 'a' in godfather.
û	pronounced as a long 'o' in the word loon.
î	long 'i' sound.
th	pronounced 'th' in that.
sh	pronunced 'sh' in show.
w	pronunced like 'w' in English.
y	pronunced like 'y' in yes.

Consonants that sound the same as their English counterparts are stressed b, d, f, k, l, m, n, s, t, and z. When these stressed consonants are followed by a, the a is pronounced as the a in car.

Difficult Arabic letters

q	'a' 'k' sound pronunced deep in the throat.
kh	pronounced like a hard 'ch' in bunch.
gh	pronunced like a rolled 'r'.
ᶜ	a sound that comes deep from the throat.
'	no sound but a pause in words.

Phrases for school

How are you? . . . . Kef Halek?
Did you finish your homework? . . . . Ameleti Wajbek?
What tests do you have today? . . . . Shoo Fi Andakmtehan elyoum?
Welcome! . . . . aHeLeen!
Nice to meet you. . . . . Etsharfna
Welcome to our school. . . . . Ahlen wa saHlan.
My name is _____. . . . . Ana esmi _____.
What is your name? . . . . Shoo esmak?
Do you understand the teacher? . . . . Enti Faham shoo eL moalem beltki?
You need to turn in your homework everyday. . . . . Lazem teamali wajbek kel youm.
Do you have any questions? . . . . Andek sueal?
Where are you from? . . . . Men wan ente?
Do you have any brothers or sisters? . . . . Andek okot?
How are you adjusting to our school? . . . . Enti Betllebi eL madrasa?
Do you speak English? . . . . Enti tetklam english?
Do you play any sports? . . . . Shoo Betleakbi Ryada?
Do you have a girlfriend/boyfriend? . . . . Andak Habeeb/Habeeba?
What is your favorite subject in school? . . . . Shoo BetHabi belel madrsa?
What is your worst subject in school? . . . . Shoo MaBetHabi lebel madrsa?
Where is your homework? . . . . Wain wajbek?
Don't be late to class! . . . . La etkoni metakra ala saf!
Please study tonight. . . . . Bedee adrosi elyoum?
What test are you taking? . . . . Emtaltan shoo Andek?
Do you need help? . . . . Enta badak mosada?
May I help you? . . . . Badak a sadek?
Please pay attention. . . . . Arjokom Intibho.
Good work! . . . . Jead!
Do you understand the test? . . . . Enti Fahama el emteHan?
Do you understand your homework? . . . . Enti Fahama Wajabak?
I am proud of you. . . . . Ana FaHora Feek.
Keep up the good work. . . . . Koni shatra alatool.
Do you know where your next class is? . . . . Betarafi wain safek?
How was art class? . . . . Kef Saf al resam?
How was gym class? . . . . Kef Saf al ryada?
How was music class? . . . . Kef Saf al music?
Quiet please. . . . . Hodoa.
Please don't interrupt. . . . . Arja eL Hodoo
You need to write a descriptive essay. . . . . Anta lasem toktob al moduaw.
Happy Birthday! . . . . Eeid milad saaeed!
Peace. . . . . Salam.

Common words and phrases

Hello . . . . Ahalan
Goodbye. . . . . Maa ElSalama
Please . . . . Min Fadilak
Excuse me . . . . Ann Eazinak
Thank you . . . . Shokran
You're welcome. . . . . Ala ElRahib Wa ElSaa
Nice to meet you. . . . . For a Saeede
Good morning. . . . . Sabaa AlKair
Good afternoon. . . . . Masaa AlKair
Good evening . . . . Masaa AlKair

Good night . . . . .TessbeH ALKair
No . . . . .Laa
Maybe . . . . .Yim Kin
Open. . . . . .Maftouh
Closed. . . . . Mogilag
All . . . . Kol
A little. . . . . Kalil
A lot . . . . Kathir
Good. . . . . Taib/Bikair
Bad . . . . Saia/Mosh Bikair

Questions
Who?. . . . . Meen?
What? . . . . 'Eyh?
When?. . . . . 'Imta?
Where? . . . . Feyn?
Why?. . . . . Leyh?
How? . . . . Izzayy/keuf?
How much?. . . . . Kam? bi kam?
Where is _____?. . . . . Ain _____?
What is this? . . . . Ma Hatha?
I do not understand.. . . . . Ana laa Afham
How do you say this in English?. . . . . . Kaif Takool Thalik Bil?
Do you speak English? . . . . Hal Takakalm Alinglizia?
What is your name?. . . . . Ma Ismok?
How are you? . . . . Kaifa Halok?
How much does this cost? . . . . Bikam?
I will buy it. . . . . Saashtariha.
I would like to buy _____ . . . . Oreed ann ashtary _____.
Do you have _____? . . . . Hal aindak _____?
Do you accept credit cards? . . . . Hal takibal bitakit el aitiman?
What time is it?. . . . . kam Al saaa?

Where
Where's the bathroom? . . . . Ain Alhamaam?
Where is _____?. . . . . Ain _____?
Airport . . . . Matar
Train station. . . . . Mahatit Al kitar
Bus station . . . . Mahatit Al Autobees
Subway station . . . . Mahatit Al Metro
Car rental agency . . . . Shirkat Taigir Sahiarat
Hotel. . . . . Fondok
Post office. . . . . Markaz Barid
Bank . . . . Bank
Police station . . . . Kissam Shorta
Hospital . . . . Mostashifa
Drug store/Pharmacy . . . . Saydaleeya
Store, Shop. . . . . Mahaal
Restaurant . . . . MaTam
School. . . . . Madrassa
Church . . . . Kanisa
Restrooms . . . . Hamam, toilets
Left . . . . Shimal

Right . . . . amain
Far . . . . Baaid
Near . . . . Karib

Who

Mother . . . . Om
Father . . . . Ab
Brother . . . . Akhkh (Singular),
                    ikhweht (Plural)
Sister . . . . Ukht
Family . . . . Eyla/Usra
Wife . . . . Zaoga
Husband . . . . Zaog
Daughter . . . . Ibna
Son . . . . Ibn
Friend . . . . Sadik
Teacher . . . . Mudaris/mudarrisa
Student . . . . Taalib/Taaliba
Doctor . . . . Tabeeb/duktoor
Policeman . . . . Askaree
Waiter . . . . Mitr

I . . . . Ana
We . . . . Nahono
You (singular) . . . . Anta (M), Anti (F)
You (plural) . . . . Antom, Antona
They . . . . Hom (M), Hoonna (F)

What

Train . . . . Kitar
Bus . . . . Autobees
Room . . . . Korfa
Reservation . . . . Hagiz
Passport . . . . Gawaz Safar
Ticket . . . . Tathkara
Map . . . . Karita
Tourist information . . . . Mailomat al Saih
Postcard . . . . Kart Barid
Stamps . . . . Tawabia
May I have the menu, please? . . . . Iddeenee ilminyu min faDlak?
Please bring the check. . . . . El Fatora Min Fadilak.
Breakfast . . . . iftar
Lunch . . . . Gadaa
Dinner . . . . Ashaa
Coffee . . . . Kahioa
Tea . . . . Shai
Milk . . . . Laban/Haleeb
Juice . . . . Asir
Water . . . . Maa
Bread . . . . Kobiz
Fruit . . . . Fawakih
Salad . . . . Salata
Beef . . . . Lahim
Pork . . . . Lahim kanzir

Fish . . . . Samak
Chicken . . . . Firehkh/Dajehj
Vegetable . . . . Kodrawat
Dessert . . . . Halawiaat
Salt . . . . Malih
Pepper . . . . Filfil

When

Today . . . . Al youm
Yesterday . . . . Amis
Tomorrow . . . . Bokira
Now . . . . Dilwatee
Minute . . . . Daeea
Hour . . . . Seha
Arrive . . . . Yiw Sal
Depart . . . . Yimshee

Day . . . . Youm
Week . . . . Isboo
Month . . . . Sahir
Year . . . . SanaaAmm

Monday . . . . Al Ithinin
Tuesday . . . . Al Tholathaa
Wednesday . . . . Al Arbiaa
Thursday . . . . Al Kamis
Friday . . . . Al Gomiaa
Saturday . . . . Al Sabit
Sunday . . . . Al Ahad

January . . . . Yanair
February . . . . Febrair
March . . . . Maris
April . . . . Apreel
May . . . . Mayo
June . . . . Yonia
July . . . . Yolia
August . . . . Aagostos
September . . . . Septamber
October . . . . Octobar
November . . . . Novamber
December . . . . Disamiber

Fall . . . . Karif
Winter . . . . Shita'a
Spring . . . . Al Rabi'a
Summer . . . . Al Sai'if

How many

zero . . . . sifer
one . . . . wahid
two . . . . ithinin
three . . . . thalatha
four . . . . arbaa
five . . . . kamisa
six . . . . sita
seven . . . . sabaa
eight . . . . thamania
nine . . . . tisaa
ten . . . . ashara

eleven . . . . hidashar
twelve . . . . itnashar
thirteen . . . . talatashar
fourteen . . . . arbatashar
fifteen . . . . kamastashar
sixteen . . . . sitashar
seventeen . . . . sabatashar
eighteen . . . . tamantashar
nineteen . . . . tisatashar
twenty . . . . ishrin

twenty one . . . . wahid wa ishrin
thirty . . . . talatin
forty . . . . arbaain
fifty . . . . kamisin
sixty . . . . sitin
seventy . . . . sabaain
eighty . . . . tamanin
ninety . . . . tisain
one hundred . . . . miaa

Brazilian Portuguese

Brazilian Portuguese is used by 190 million people in Brazil. There is a formal written and spoken version of Portuguese taught in schools throughout Brazil. Brazilian Portuguese is very similar to European Portuguese, but there are many differences in spelling, word usage and grammar. Informal spoken version varies widely. In a country as large and diverse as Brazil, "correct" pronunciation is often a matter of who is speaking, where they come from and/or where one happens to be.

Vowels

a	pronounced like the 'a' in father
e	variously pronounced either like the 'ay' in say or the 'e' in bet
i	pronounced like the 'ee' in meet
o	pronounced like the 'o' in vote
u	pronounced like the 'oo' in boot

Consonants

b	pronounced much like English
c	pronounced like the 'c' in coin or 's' in safe
ç	pronounced like the 's' in several
d	pronounced like English except before 'i' or 'e' where it is pronounced like the 'dj' in judge
g	pronounced like the hard 'g' in got or soft 'g' sound in pleasure
h	silent except when followed by an 'n' where it creates the nasal sound similar to the Spanish 'ñ' as in señor
j	pronounced like the 'dj' sound in measure
k	pronounced like the 'k' in kite
l	pronounced like English except it tends to nasalize the vowel preceeding it — when following an 'a' or 'i' as the last letter of a word it takes on a 'w' sound
m	pronounced like English except it tends to nasalize the vowel preceeding it — when the last letter of a word pronounced without closing the lips at the end — like an n
n	pronounced like English except it tends to nasalize the vowel preceeding it
r	as the first letter of a word – pronounced like a nasalized h in heat-----inside a word pronounced much like English-----at the end a word – pronounced somewhat gutterally
s	between vowels pronounced like the 'z' sound in rose, otherwise liike the 's' in satisfaction
t	pronounced like English except when follwed by an 'e 'or (especially) an 'i' when it is pronounced like the 'chee' in cheese
v	pronounced like English
w	Brazilians tend to pronounce like 'a' 'v', for example, Walter becomes Valter
x	variously pronounced like the 'sh' in shed (e.g. xuxa = shoe-sha), the 's' in seen or the 'x' in taxi
y	pronounced like the 'y' in yell or the 'ee' sound in funny
z	pronounced like the 'z' in zero

Phrases for school

English	Portuguese
How are you?	Como vai você?
Did you finish your homework?	Você terminou sua tarefa de casa?
What tests do you have today?	Que testes você tem hoje?
Welcome.	Bem-vindo (M), Bem-vinda (F)
Nice to meet you.	Muito prazer.
Welcome to our school.	Bem-vindo a nossa escola (M) / Bem-vinda a nossa escola (F)
My name is _____.	Meu nome é _____.
What is your name?	Qual é o seu nome?
Do you understand the teacher?	Você entende o professor?(M) / Você entende a professora?(F)
You need to turn in your homework everyday.	Você precisa trazer sua tarefa de casa todos os dias.
Do you have any questions?	Você tem perguntas?
Where are you from?	De onde você é?
Do you have any brothers or sisters?	Você tem irmãos?
How are you adjusting to our school?	Como você está se acostumando com a nossa escola?
Do you speak English?	Você fala inglês?
Do you play any sports?	Você pratica algum esporte?
Do you have a girlfriend/boyfriend?	Você tem um namorado? (M) / Você tem uma namorada? (F)
What is your favorite subject in school?	Qual é a sua matéria favorita na escola?
Where is your homework?	Onde está a sua tarefa de casa?
Don't be late to class!	Não se atrase para a aula!
Please study tonight.	Por favor, estude hoje a noite.
What test are you taking?	Que prova você está fazendo?
Do you need help?	Você precisa de ajuda?
May I help you?	Eu posso te ajudar?
Please pay attention.	Por favor, preste atenção.
Good work!	Bom trabalho!
Do you understand the test?	Você entende o teste?
Do you understand your homework?	Você entende a sua tarefa de casa?
I am proud of you.	Eu estou orgulhoso de você. (M) / Eu estou orgulhosa de você. (F)
Keep up the good work.	Continue fazendo um bom trabalho.
Do you know where your next class is?	Você sabe onde será a sua próxima aula?
How was art class?	Como foi a aula de artes?
How was gym class?	Como foi a aula de educação física?
How was music class?	Como foi a aula de música?
Quiet please.	Silêncio, por favor.
Please don't interrupt.	Não interrompa por favor!

You need to write a descriptive essay. . . . . Você precisa de escrever uma dissertação descritiva.

You need to write a narrative paper. . . . . Você precisa de escrever uma narrativa.

You need to write a comparison/contrast paper. . . . Você precisa de escrever um documento comparativo.

You need to write a poem. . . . . Você precisa escrever um poema.

The homework is due_____ . . . . Sua tarefa de casa é para _____.

The test is _____ . . . . O teste é _____.

Your project is due _____ . . . . Seu projeto é para _____.

Your paper is due _____ . . . . Seu documento é para _____.

There is no school tomorrow. . . . . Não haverá aula amanhã.

Happy Birthday! . . . . Feliz Aniversário!

Common words and phrases

Hello . . . . Oi

Goodbye . . . . Tchau, Até logo

Please . . . . Por favor

Excuse me . . . . Com lincença

Thank you . . . . Obrigado (M), Obrigada (F)

You're welcome . . . . De nada

Nice to meet you. . . . . Muito prazer.

Good morning . . . . Bom dia

Good afternoon . . . . Boa tarde

Good evening . . . . Boa noite

Good night . . . . Boa noite

Yes . . . . Sim

No . . . . Não

Maybe . . . . Talvez

Open . . . . Aberto (M)/Aberta (F)

Closed . . . . Fechado (M)/Fechada (F)

All . . . . Todo (M)/Toda (F)

A little . . . . Um pouco de

A lot . . . . Muito (M)/Muita (F)

Good . . . . Bom (M)/Boa (F)

Bad . . . . Mau (M)/Má (F)

Questions

Who? . . . . Quem?

What? . . . . O quê?

When? . . . . Quando?

Where? . . . . Onde?

How? . . . . Como?

How much? . . . . Quanto/Quanta?(Singular), Quantos/Quantas?(Plural)

Where is _____? . . . . Onde é?

What is this? . . . . O quê é isso?

I do not understand. . . . . Eu não entendo.

How do you say this in English? . . . . Como você fala isto em inglês?

Do you speak English? . . . . Você fala inglês?

What is your name? . . . . Qual é o seu nome?

How are you? . . . . Como vai você?

How much does this cost? . . . . Quanto custa isto?

I will buy it. . . . . Eu comprarei isto.

I would like to buy_____ . . . . Eu gostaria de comprar _____.

Do you have _____?. . . . . Você tem ____?

Do you accept credit cards? . . . . Você aceita cartão de crédito?

What time is it? . . . . Que horas são?

Where

Where's the bathroom? . . . . Onde está o banheiro? Onde está a toalete?

Where is ____? . . . . Onde está ____ ?

Subway . . . . Metrô

Airport . . . . Aeroporto

Train station . . . . Estação de trem

Bus station . . . . Ponto de ônibus

Subway station . . . . Estação de metrô

Car rental agency . . . . Agência de aluguel de carros

Hotel . . . . Hotel

Post office . . . . Correio

Bank . . . . Banco

Police station . . . . Delegacia Policial

Hospital . . . . Hospital

Pharmacy . . . . Farmácia

Store . . . . Loja

Restaurant . . . . Restaurante

School . . . . Escola

Church . . . . Igreja

Restrooms . . . . Banheiros

Left . . . . Esquerda

Right . . . . Direita

Far . . . . Longe

Near . . . . Perto

Who

Mother . . . . Mãe

Father . . . . Pai

Brother . . . . Irmão

Sister . . . . Irmã

Family . . . . Família

Wife . . . . Esposa

Husband . . . . Esposo

Son . . . . Filho

Daughter . . . . Filha

Friend . . . . Amigo (M) / Amiga (F)

Teacher . . . . Professor (M)/Professora (F)

Student . . . . Estudante
Doctor . . . . Médico (M)/Médica (F)
Policeman . . . . Policial

I . . . . Eu
We . . . . Nós
You (singular) . . . . Você
You (plural) . . . . Vocês
They . . . . Eles (M)/Elas (F)

What
Train . . . . Trem
Bus . . . . Ônibus
Room . . . . Quarto
Reservation . . . . Reserva
Passport . . . . Passaporte
Ticket . . . . Passagem
Map . . . . Mapa
Tourist information . . . . Informação de Turista
Postcard . . . . Cartão Postal
Stamps . . . . Selos
May I see a menu, please? . . . . . Eu gostaria de ver o cardápio, por favor?
I would like to order. . . . . Eu gostaria de pedir.
Please bring the check. . . . . A conta, por favor.
Breakfast . . . . Café da manhã
Lunch . . . . Almoço
Dinner . . . . Jantar
Beverage . . . . Bebida
Coffee . . . . Café
Milk . . . . Leite
Tea . . . . Chá
Juice . . . . Suco
Water . . . . Água
Wine . . . . Vinho
Bread . . . . Pão
Beef . . . . Bife
Pork . . . . Carne de porco
Fish . . . . Peixe
Chicken . . . . Carne de frango
Vegetable . . . . Legume
Fruit . . . . Fruta
Salad . . . . Salada
Dessert . . . . Sobremesa
Salt . . . . Sal
Pepper . . . . Pimenta

When

Today	Hoje
Yesterday	Ontem
Tomorrow	Amanhã
Now	Agora
Minute	Minuto
Hour	hora
Arrive	Chegar
Depart	Partir

Day	Dia
Week	Semana
Month	Mês
Year	Ano

Monday	Segunda-feira
Tuesday	Terça-feira
Wednesday	Quarta-feira
Thursday	Quinta-feira
Friday	Sexta-feira
Saturday	Sábado
Sunday	Domingo

January	Janeiro
February	Fevereiro
March	Março
April	Abril
May	Maio
June	Junho
July	Julho
August	Agosto
September	Setembro
October	Outubro
November	Novembro
December	Dezembro

Fall	Outono
Winter	Inverno
Spring	Primavera
Summer	Verão

How many

zero	zero
one	um (M), uma (F)
two	dois (M), duas (F)
three	três
four	quatro
five	cinco
six	seis
seven	sete
eight	oito
nine	nove
ten	dez

eleven	onze
twelve	doze
thirteen	treze
fourteen	catorze or quatorze
fifteen	quinze
sixteen	dezesseis
seventeen	dezessete
eighteen	dezoito
nineteen	dezenove
twenty	vinte

twenty one	vinte e um
thirty	trinta
forty	quarenta
fifty	cinquenta
sixty	sessenta
seventy	setenta
eighty	oitenta
ninety	noventa
one hundred	cem

Chinese - Mandarin

The official Chinese language is Mandarin, and Beijing Mandarin constitutes the standard dialect called Putonghua. Mandarin Chinese is a tonal language spoken by more than one billion people in China, Taiwan and Singapore. There is also a significant number of Mandarin speakers in Malaysia, Indonesia, Russia, the USA, Mongolia, Vietnam, Brunei, South Africa, Thailand, Laos, Cambodia, Hong Kong, the Philippines, UK and Mauritius.

Consonants

Consonants cannot exist without a vowel or a diphthong. The consonants when read individually, except j, q, x, zh, ch, sh, r, z, c, s should be read as consonant sound plus schwa (a neutral vowel). The exceptions are read as consonant sound + short 'i '(as in big).

b	unaspirated p	p	aspirated p
m	as in mother	f	as in father
d	unaspirated t	t	aspirated t
n	as in nose	l	as in luck
g	unaspirated k	k	aspirated k
h	as in house	j	unaspirated ts as is tu in capture
q	aspirated ts	x	as in soft s
Zh	unaspirated ch	ch	aspirated ch as in the English ch
Sh	as in show	r	r
z	unaspirated sharp dz	c	aspirated sharp dz
s	a hard s, a sound between s and z		

Vowels and Dipthongs

Vowels and dipthongs can be separated from a consonant.

a	as in star	ê	as in pen
ai	as in eye	ei	as ay in say
ao	as ou in how	en	schwa + n
an	as in a in bar + n	o	as in long
e	as in the schwa	ou	long o as in code

Phrases for school

How are you?	Ni hao ma?
Did you finish your homework?	Ni zuo wan zuo ye le ma?
What tests do you have today?	Jin tian ni you shen ma kao shi?
Welcome	Huan ying.
Nice to meet you.	Hen gao xing jian dao ni.
Welcome to our school.	Huan ying lai wo men xue xiao.
My name is _____.	Wo de ming zi shi _____.
What is your name?	Nin gui xing?
Do you understand the teacher?	Ni dong lao shi de hua ma?
You need to turn in your homework everyday.	Ni mei tian dou yao jiao zuo ye.
Do you have any questions?	Ni you wen ti ma?
Where are you from?	Ni Cong na lai?
Do you have any brothers or sisters?	Ni you xiong di jie mei ma?
How are you adjusting to our school?	Ni Shi ying wo men xue xiao ma?
Do you speak English?	Ni shuo ying yu ma?
Do you play any sports?	Xi huan ti yu huo dong ma?
Do you have a girlfriend/boyfriend?	Ni you nan peng you ma?
	Ni you nyu peng you ma?
What is your favorite subject in school?	Ni zui xi huan xue xiao zhong na men gong ke?
What is your worst subject in school?	Ni zui bu xi huan xue xiao zhong na men gong ke?
Where is your homework?	Ni de zuo ye zai na?
Don't be late to class!	Bu yao chi dao!
Please study tonight.	Jin wan qing xue xi.
What test are you taking?	Ni zai kao shen ma?
Do you need help?	Xu yao bang zhu ma?
May I help you?	Wo ke yi bang ni ma?
Please pay attention.	Qing ji zhong jing li.
Good work!	Zuo de hen hao!
Do you understand the test?	Kao shi ti ni dong ma?
Do you understand your homework?	Zuo ye ni dong ma?
I am proud of you.	Wo wei ni gan dao jiao ao.
Keep up the good work.	Ji xu nu li.
Do you know where your next class is?	Ni zhi dao xia jie ke zai na ma?
How was art class?	Yi shu ke zen me yang?
How was gym class?	Ti cao ke zen me yang?
How was music class?	Yin yue ke zen me yang?
Quiet please.	Qing an jing.
Please don't interrupt.	Qing bie da rao.
You need to write a descriptive essay.	Ni xu yao xie yi pian miao shu xing de wen zhang.
The homework is due _____	Jiao zuo ye de ri zi shi _____.
Your test is _____.	Ni de kao shi shi _____.
Your project is due _____	Ni jiao xiang mu de ri zi shi _____.
You need to write a paper	Ni ying xie yi ge zhi.
You need to write a research paper	Ni ying xie yi ge yan jiu.
Do you have any questions?	Ni you wen ti ma?
Happy Birthday!	sheng ri kuai le!

Common words and phrases

Hello . . . . .ni hao
Goodbye . . . . .zai jian
Please . . . . .qing
Excuse me . . . . .qing rang, dui bu qi
Thank you . . . . .xie xie
You're welcome .bu yong xie
Nice to meet you. . . . . .hen gao xing yu jian ni.
Good morning .zao an
Good afternoon .wu an
Good evening . . . . .wan shang hao
Good night . . . . .wan an
Yes . . . . .shi
No . . . . .bu shi
Maybe . . . . .dagai, yexu
Open . . . . .kai
Closed . . . . .guan
All . . . . .quan bu
A little . . . . .yi dian er
A lot . . . . .hen duo
Good . . . . .hao
Bad . . . . .bu hao

Questions

Who? . . . . .shei?
What? . . . . .shenme?
When? . . . . .shenme shihou?
Where? . . . . .nali?
How? . . . . .zenme?
How much? . . . . .duo shao?
Where is _____? .zai na li?
What is this? . . . . .zhe shi shen me?
I do not understand. . . . . .wo bu ming bai/wo bu dong
How do you say this in English? . . . . . . .zhe yong ying yu zen me jiang?
Do you speak English? . . . . .ni jiang ying yu ma?
What is your name? . . . . .ni jiao shen me ming zi?
How are you? . . . . .ni hao ma?
How much does this cost? . . . . .zhe duo shao qian?
What is this? . . . . .zhe shi shen me?
I will buy it. . . . . .wo mai.
I would like to buy _____ . . . . .wo yao mai _____.
Do you have _____? . . . . .ni you mei you _____?
Do you accept credit cards? . . . . .ni jie shou xǐn yong ka ma?
What's the time? . . . . .ji dian le?

Where

Where's the bathroom? . . . . .xi shou jian zai na li?
Where is _____? .zai na li?
Airport . . . . .fei ji chang
Train station . . . . .huo che zhan
Bus station . . . . .gong che zhan
Subway station .di tie zhan
Car rental agency . . . . .chu zu qi che zhang

Hotel . . . . .lu guan
Post office . . . . .you ju
Bank . . . . .yin hang
Police station .jing cha ju
Hospital . . . . .yi yuan
Drug Store/Pharmacy . . . . .yao fang
Grocery store/Store . . . . .dian
Restaurant . . . . .jiu lou/Fan guan
School . . . . .xue xiao
Church . . . . .jiao tang
Restrooms . . . . .xi shou jian
Left . . . . .zuo
Right . . . . .you
Far . . . . .yuan
Near . . . . .jin

Who
Mother . . . . .ma ma
Father . . . . .ba ba
Brother . . . . .xiongdi
Sister . . . . .jiejie/jie mei
Family . . . . .jiating
Wife . . . . .qi zi
Husband . . . . .zhang fu
Son . . . . .er zi
Daughter . . . . .nu er
Friend . . . . .peng you
Teacher . . . . .jiaoshi/lao shi
Student . . . . .xue sheng
Doctor . . . . .yisheng
Policeman . . . . .jingcha
Waiter . . . . .fuwuyuan

I . . . . .wo
We . . . . .wo men
You (singular) . . . . .ni/nin
You (plural) . . . . .ni men
They . . . . .ta men

What
Train . . . . .huo che
Bus . . . . .gong che
Room . . . . .ke fang
Reservation . . . . .yu ding
Passport . . . . .hu zhao
Ticket . . . . .piao
Map . . . . .di tu
Tourist information . . . . .lu you wen xun chu
Postcard . . . . .ming xin pian
Stamps . . . . .you piao
May l have the check please?. . . . . .qing jie zhang?
Breakfast . . . . .zao can
Lunch . . . . .wu can

Dinner ....wan can
Coffee ....ka fei
Tea ....cha
Milk ....niunai
Juice ....guo zhi
Water ....shui
Bread ....mian bao
Fruit ....shiu guo
Salad ....sa la
Beef ....niu rou
Pork ....zhu rou
Fish ....yu
Chicken ....ji rou
Vegetable ....cai
Dessert ....dian xin
Salt ....yan
Pepper ....hu jiao

When
Today ....jin tian
Yesterday ....zuo tian
Tomorrow ....ming tian
Now ....xianzai
Minute ....fenzhong
Hour ....xiaoshi
Depart ....chu jing
Arrive ....ru jing

Day ....ri/tian
Week ....xing qi
Month ....yue
Year ....nian

Monday ....xing qi yi
Tuesday ....xing qi er
Wednesday ....xing qi san
Thursday ....xing qi si
Friday ....xing qi wu
Saturday ....xing qi liu
Sunday ....xing qi ri

January ....yi yue
February ....er yue
March ....san yue
April ....si yue
May ....wu yue

June ....liu yue
July ....qi yue
August ....ba yue
September ....jiu yue
October ....shi yue
November ....shi yi yue
December ....shi er yue

Fall ....qiu
Winter ....dong
Spring ....chun
Summer ....xia

How many
zero ....ling
one ....yi
two ....er
three ....san
four ....si
five ....wu
six ....liu
seven ....qi
eight ....ba
nine ....jiu
ten ....shi

eleven ....shi yi
twelve ....shi er
thirteen ....shi san
fourteen ....shi si
fifteen ....shi wu
sixteen ....shi liu
seventeen ....shi qi
eighteen ....shi ba
nineteen ....shi jiu
twenty ....er shi

twenty one ....er shi yi
thirty ....san shi
forty ....si shi
fifty ....wu shi
sixty ....liu shi
seventy ....qi shi
eighty ....ba shi
ninety ....jiu shi
one hundred ....yi bai

Farsi

Farsi is also known as Persian, spoken in the Middle East and central Asia. Its dialects include Dari (Afghanistan) and Tajik (Tajistan). It is a language spoken in Iran, Tajikistan, Afghanistan, Uzbekistan, Bahrain, Iraq, Azerbaijan, Armenia and Southern Russia. It belongs to the Indo-European language family, and it is of the Subject-Object-Verb type. There are over 61 million native speakers of Farsi in Iran, Afghanistan, Tajikistan and Uzbekistan.

There are six vowels and 23 consonants.

Pronunciation

In dictionary	Sounds like
a	'a' in sad
â (aa)	'a' in stall
e	'e' in bed
I	'ea' in sea
ei	'ai' in brain
o	'o' in carrot
u	'oo' in loot
ow	'ow' in blow
'	stop or pause
zh	's' in measure
kh	'ch' in German for Bach
q	similar to 'k' sound made back in the throat
v	'v' in victory

Phrases for school

How are you?	Hall shoma cheToreh?
Did you finish your homework?	Shoma mashgheTan ra tamam kardid?
What tests do you have today?	Emros shoma Che emTehani darid ?
Welcome.	Khosh amadid.
Nice to meet you.	Az molagat shoma khosh halla'm.
Welcome to our school.	Be madresay ma Kosh amadid.
My name is _____.	Esme man hast _____.
What is your name?	Esme shoma cheieh?
Do you understand the teacher?	Shoma harf moalem ra mefahmid?
You need to turn in your homework everyday.	Shoma bayad har rooz taklifetan ra anjam dahid.
Do you have any questions?	Soalli darid?
Where are you from?	Shoma ahll koga hastide?
Do you have any brothers or sisters?	Shoma kaher ya baradar darid?
How are you adjusting to our school?	Be madreseh a'dat Kardi?
Do you speak English?	Shoma englisy sohbaTmeKonid?
Do you play any sports?	Shoma warzesh mekonid?
Do you have a girlfriend/boyfriend?	Shoma doust dokhtar ya doust pesar darid?
What is your favorite subject in school?	Che darsi ra doust darid?
What is your worst subject in school?	Che darsi ra doust nadarid?
Where is your homework?	Mashgh shoma Koja ast?
Don't be late to class!	Be class deer naiied/Takheer Nakonid!
Please study tonight.	LoTfan emshab moTale Konid.
What test are you taking?	Che emtehany ra meedin?
Do you need help?	Shoma komak mekhahid?
May I help you?	Momkene be shoma comak Konam?
Please pay attention.	Lotfan Tavajoh konid.
Good work!	Caret khobe!
Do you understand the test?	Shoma emtehan ra mefahmid?
Do you understand your homework?	Taklifetan ra mefahmid?
I am proud of you.	Man be shoma eftekhar mikonam.
Keep up the good work.	In kare khob ra edameh bedeh.
Do you know where your next class is?	Classe badie shoma kojast?
How was art class?	Classe honar chetor bood?
How was gym class?	Classe vwarzesh chetor bood?
How was music class?	Classe mouseghi chetor bood?
Quiet please.	Lotfan Saket bashid.
Please don't interrupt.	Saket, Ejaze bedeh.
The homework (paper) is due _____.	Taklifetan ra bayd anjam dahid _____.
The test is_____.	Emtehanetan hast _____.
Your project is due _____	In porjeh ra anjam dahid _____.
Your paper is due _____	Taklifetan ra bayd bedahid.
There is no school tomorrow.	Farda/madrese tatileh.
Where are you going?	Shoma Koja Miravid?
Where do you live?	Shoma Koja Zandegi Mikonid?
Happy Birthday!	Tavalodat Mobarak!

Common words and phrases

Hello	Salam
Goodbye	Khoda Hafez
Please	Khahesh Mikonam/loTfan
Excuse me	Mazerat Mikham
Thank you	Merci or moteshakeram
You're welcome	Khosh Amadid, ghabel nadareh
Nice to meet you.	As didar shoma Khoshhalm
Good morning	Sobh Bekhear
Good afternoon	Bad az Zohr Bekhayr
Good evening	Shab Behkhayr
Good night	Shab Behkhayr
Yes	Baleh
No	Nah
Maybe	Shayad, momkene
All	Hameh/Tamam
Good	Khob
Bad	Bad

Questions

Who?	Ki/Che-Kasi?
What?	Cheh? (chi)?
When?	Keiy?
Where?	Koja?
Why?	Chera?
How?	Chegoone/Chejoori/Chetowr?
How much?	Chand/Cheqadar?
Where is _____?	Koja Hast _____?
What is this?	In Chieeh?
I do not understand..	Man Nemefahmam.
How do you say this in English?	In Beh englisy Cheh Mishe?
Do you speak English?	Shoma Engalisi Sohbat Mekonid?
What is your name?	Esmeh Shoma Cheeh?
How are you?	Haleton Chetoreh?
How much does this cost?	Ghaematesh Chande or Che ghaymate?
I will buy it.	Man In Ra Mikharam.
I would like to buy _____.	Man doust daram In Ra Bakharam.
Do you have _____?	Shoma Darid?
Do you accept credit cards?	Shoma Credit Card Ghabol Mikonid?
What time is it?	Saat Chandeh?

Where

Where's the bathroom? Where is the toilet?	Toalet Kojast? Dastshoei Kojast?
Where is _____?	Koja Hast _____?
Airport	Forodgah
Train station	Istgah Tran
Bus station	Istgah Autobus
Subway station	Istgah Tran Zir Zamini/metro
Car rental agency	Ajance Krayeh Mashin
Hotel	Hotel
Post office	Postkhaneh
Bank	Bank
Hospital	Marizkhaneh
Drug Store/Pharmacy	Darokhaneh
Grocery store/Store	Moghazeh/souper market
Restaurant	Restauran
School	Madreseh
Church	Kalleseaa
Restrooms	Toalet/dastshoei
Left	Chap
Right	Rast
Near	Nazdik

Who

Mother	Madar/maman
Father	Pedar
Brother	Baradar
Sister	Khahar
Family	Khanevadeh
Husband	Shohar
Wife	Zan
Son	Pesar
Daughter	Dokhtar
Friend	Rafigh/doust
Teacher	Mo-allem/amoozegar
Student	Shagerd/Mohassel/Danesh-amooz

I	Man
We	Ma
You (singular)	Tou, Shoma
You (plural)	Shoma
They	Anha

What

Train	Tran
Bus	Autobus
Room	Otagh
Reservation	Reserv
Passport	Passport
Ticket	Bilit
Map	Naghsheh
Tourist information	Etelate touristi
Postcard	Cartpostal
Stamps	Tamr
Please bring the check.	Lotfan Hesabe ra Biavarid.
Breakfast	Sobhaneh
Lunch	Nahar
Dinner	Sham
Coffee	Ghahveh
Tea	Chayee
Milk	Shir
Juice	Abmiveh
Water	Ab
Bread	Nan
Fruit	Miveh
Salad	Salad
Beef	Goshtee Gav
Pork	Goshtee Khok
Fish	Mahi
Chicken	Morgh
Vegetable	Sabzi
Dessert	Deser
Salt	Namak
Pepper	Felfel
Beer	Abjo
Wine	Sharab

When

Today	EmRooz
Yesterday	Diroz
Tomorrow	Farda
Now	Al-an/Hala/Aknoon
Minute	Daghigheh
Hour	Sa'at
Arrive	Vorod
Depart	Khoroj
Day	Rooz
Week	Hafteh
Month	Mahh
Year	Saal

Monday	Do Shambeh
Tuesday	Seh Shambeh
Wednesday	Chahar Shambeh
Thursday	Panj Shambeh
Friday	Jomeh
Saturday	Shambeh
Sunday	Yek Shambeh

January	Janveeeh
February	Febreeeh
March	March
April	Avreel
May	May
June	Juan
July	July
August	Oout
September	Septambr
October	Octobr
November	Novambr
December	Desambr

Fall	Payez
Winter	Zemestan
Spring	Bahar
Summer	Tabestan

How Many

zero	sefr
one	yek
two	dow
three	seh
four	chahar
five	panj
six	shesh
seven	haft
eight	hasht
nine	noh
ten	dah

eleven	yazdah
twelve	davazdah
thirteen	sizdah
fourteen	chardah
fifteen	ponzdah
sixteen	shonzdah
seventeen	hafdah
eighteen	hejdah
nineteen	nozdah
twenty	beast

twenty one	beastoyek
thirty	see
forty	chahel
fifty	panjah
sixty	shast
seventy	haftad
eighty	hashtad
ninety	navad
one hundred	saad

French

French is a language shaped by centuries of Roman rule, a Romance language. French has been an important language in Europe since the seventeenth century. It remains a major language today as an official language of the UN and 29 countries. French is prevalent in parts of Belgium, parts of Switzerland, eastern Canada (especially in Quebec and New Brunswick), Luxembourg, Monaco, parts of Africa (Algeria, Ivory Coast, Republic of the Congo, Morocco, Niger, Senegal and Tunisia), Haiti, Mauritius, and Southeast Asia (such as Laos and Vietnam).

Many English words derive from French, and America's culture has been greatly influenced by the settlers of New Orleans and Louisiana. Many recent immigrants come from French-speaking countries.

Consonants

Many French consonants are not pronounced. However, b, d, f, k, l, m, n, p, t, v, y, and z are pronounced as in English.

c	pronounced as 's'.
A	pronounced as 's' and only occurs before a, o, and u.
ch	is pronounced as 'sh'.
tch	'tch' as in catch.
g	pronounced as the 's' in fusion before e, i, y plus it is also pronounced as a hard 'g' in garden.
h	'h' is not pronounced.
j	's' as in vision.
ille	pronounced as 'y'.
ph	as 'f' in phone.
qu	as 'k' in quarter.
s	between the vowels it is pronounced as 'z', but at the end of the words s is usually silent.
ss	pronounced 's'.
th	is pronounced 't'.
w	pronounced 'w' as in swat.
x	x is pronounced 'ks' before most of the consonant.
y	y is pronounced 'ee' or 'y' before words beginning with the vowels.

Phrases for school

How are you? . . . . Comment allez-vous? Comment ça va? Ça va?

Did you finish your homework? . . . . Est-ce que vous avez fini vos devoirs?

What tests do you have today? . . . . Quels examens est-ce que que vous avez aujourd'hui?

Welcome . . . . Bienvenue

Nice to meet you . . . . Enchanté(e)

Welcome to our school . . . . Bienvenue à notre école

My name is _____. . . . . Je m'appelle _____.

What is your name? . . . . Comment vous appelez-vous?

Do you understand the teacher? . . . . Est-ce que vous comprenez le professeur?

You need to turn in your homework everyday . . . . Vous avez besoin de remettre vos devoirs chaque jour.

Do you have any questions? . . . . Est-ce que vous avez des questions?

Where are you from? . . . . D'où êtes-vous?

Do you have any brothers or sisters? . . . . Est-ce que vous avez des frères ou des soeurs?

How are you adjusting to our school? . . . . Est-ce que vous vous déleroullez à l'école?

Est-ce que vous vous habituez à l'école?

Do you speak English? . . . . Est-ce que vous parlez anglais? Parlez vous anglais?

Do you play any sports? . . . . Est-ce que vous jouez aux sports?

Est-ce que vous faites du sport?

Do you have a girlfriend/boyfriend? . . . . Est-ce que vous avez un(e) petit(e) ami(e)?

What is your favorite subject in school? . . . . Quel est votre sujet préféré à l'école?

Where is your homework? . . . . Où sont vos devoirs?

Don't be late to class! . . . . Ne soyez pas en retard à la classe!

Ne soyez pas en retard en cours!

Please study tonight. . . . . S'il-vous-plaît étudiez ce soir.

What test are you taking? . . . . Quel examen est-ce que vous passez?

Do you need help? . . . . Est-ce que vous avez besoin de l'aide?

Est-ce que vous avez besoin d'aide?

May I help you? . . . . Est-ce que je peux vous aider?

Please pay attention. . . . . S'il-vous-plaît faites attention.

Good work! . . . . Bon travail!

Do you understand the test? . . . . Est-ce que vous comprenez l'examen?

Do you understand your homework? . . . . Est-ce que vous comprenez vos devoirs?

I am proud of you. . . . . Je suis fier de vous.

Keep up the good work. . . . . Continuez le bon travail.

Do you know where your next class is? . . . . Est-ce que vous savez où est la prochaine classe (le prochain cours)?

How was art class? . . . . Comment était la classe (le cours) d'art?

How was gym class? . . . . Comment était la classe (le cours) d'education physique?

How was music class? . . . . Comment était la classe (le cours) de musique?

Quiet please. . . . . Silence s'il-vous-plaît.

Please don't interrupt. . . . . S'il-vous-plaît n'interrompez pas.

You need to write a descriptive essay. . . . . Vous avez besoin d'écrire (Vous devez écrire) une rédaction descriptive.

You need to write a narrative essay . . . . Vous avez besoin d'écrire (Vous devez écrire) une rédaction narrative..

You need to write a comparison/contrast paper. . . Vous avez besoin d'écrire (Vous devez écrire) une rédaction comparaison/contraste.

You need to write a poem. . . . . Vous avez besoin d'écrire (Vous devez écrire) un poème.

The homework is due _____ . . . . Il faut remettre les devoirs.

The test is _____ . . . . L'examen est _____.

Your project is due _____ . . . . Votre projet est pour _____.

Your paper is due _____ . . . . Votre rédaction doit être remise _____.

There is no school tomorrow. . . . . Il n'y a pas d'école demain.

Happy Birthday! . . . . Joyeux anniversaire!

Common phrases and words

Hello . . . . Bonjour
Goodbye . . . . Au revoir
Please . . . . S'il vous plaît
Excuse me . . . . pardon, excusez-moi
Thank you . . . . Merci
You're welcome . . . . de rien, je vous en prie
Nice to meet you. . . . . Enchanté (de faire votre connaissance).
Good morning . . . . Bonjour
Good afternoon . . . . Bon après-midi
Good evening . . . . Bonsoir
Good night . . . . Bonne nuit
Yes . . . . Oui
No . . . . Non
Maybe . . . . peut-être
Open . . . . ouvert
Closed . . . . fermé
All . . . . tout (M), toute (F)
A little . . . . un peu
A lot . . . . beaucoup
Good . . . . bien, bon
Bad . . . . mal, mauvais

Questions

Who? . . . . Qui?
What? . . . . Que?/Quoi?
When? . . . . Quand?
Where? . . . . Où?
Why? . . . . Pourquoi?
How? . . . . Comment?
How much? . . . . Combien?
Where is _____? . . . . Où est _____?

What is this?	Qu'est-ce que c'est?
I do not understand.	Je ne comprends pas
How do you say this in English?	Comment dit-on ça en anglais?
Do you speak English?	Parlez-vous ánglais?
What is your name?	Comment vous appelez-vous? Quel est votre nom?
How are you?	Comment allez-vous? Ça va?
How much does this cost?	Quel est le prix? Combien ça coûte?
I will buy it.	Je le prends.
I would like to buy ____	Je voudrais acheter ____.
Do you have ____?	Avez-vous ____. Est-ce que vous avez ____?
Do you accept credit cards?	Acceptez-vous les cartes de crédit?
What time is it?	Quelle heure est-il?

Where

Where's the bathroom? Where is the toilet?	Où sont les toilettes?
Airport	un aéroport
Subway/Metro	le métro
Train station	la gare
Bus station	la gare routière
Subway station/Metro station	la gare de métro
Car rental agency	Agence de location de voitures
Hotel	un hôtel
Post office	La poste
Bank	la banque
Police station	le poste de police, la gendarmerie
Hospital	l' hôspital
Drug store/Pharmacy	la pharmacie
Store	le magasin
Restaurant	le restaurant
School	une école
Church	une église
Restrooms	les toilettes
Left	à gauche
Right	à droite
Far	loin
Near	pres, proche

Who

Mother	la mère, maman
Father	le père, papa
Brother	le frère
Sister	la soeur
Family	la famille
Wife	une femme, une épouse
Husband	le mari
Daughter	la fille
Son	le fils
Friend	un ami (M), une amie (F)

Teacher . . . . le prof (colloquial), le professeur (high-school, middle school), le maître (M), la maîtresse (F) (elementary school)
Student . . . . l'étudiant (college, university)/l'élève (elementary, middle, high school)
Doctor . . . . le médecin
Policeman . . . . le policier

I . . . . je
We . . . . nous
You (singular) . . . . tu, vous
You (plural) . . . . vous
They . . . . ils(M), elles(F)

What
Train . . . . le train
Bus. . . . . un autobus
Room. . . . . une chambre
Reservation . . . . la réservation
Ticket . . . . le billet
Passport . . . . le passeport
Map. . . . . la carte
Tourist information . . . . Information touristique
Postcard . . . . la carte postale
Stamps . . . . des timbres
May I see a menu, please?. . . . . Est-ce que je peux voir un menu, s'il-vous-plaît?
I would like to order. . . . . J'aimerais commander.
Please bring the check.. . . . . l'addition, s'il vous plaît.
Breakfast. . . . . le petit déjeuner
Lunch . . . . le déjeuner
Dinner. . . . . le dîner
Coffee . . . . le cafè
Tea. . . . . le thé
Milk. . . . . le lait
Juice . . . . le jus
Water. . . . . de leau
Wine . . . . le vin
Bread. . . . . le pain
Fruit . . . . le fruit
Salad . . . . la salade
Beef . . . . le boeuf
Pork. . . . . le porc
Fish . . . . le poisson
Chicken. . . . . le poulet
Vegetable . . . . le légume
Dessert . . . . le dessert
Salt. . . . . le sel
Pepper . . . . le poivre

When

Today	Aujourd'hui
Yesterday	Hier
Tomorrow	Demain
Now	maintenant
Minute	la minute
Hour	l'heure
Arrive	l' arrivée
Depart	le départ
Day	Jour
Week	Semaine
Month	Mois
Year	Année
Monday	lundi
Tuesday	mardi
Wednesday	mercredi
Thursday	jeudi
Friday	vendredi
Saturday	samedi
Sunday	dimanche
January	janvier
February	fevrier
March	mars
April	avril
May	mai
June	juin
July	juillet
August	août
September	septembre
October	octobre
November	novembre
December	décembre
Fall	automne
Winter	hiver
Spring	printemps
Summer	été

How many

zero	zéro, nul
one	un(e)
two	deux
three	trois
four	quatre
five	cinq
six	six
seven	sept
eight	huit
nine	neuf
ten	dix
eleven	onze
twelve	douze
thirteen	treize
fourteen	quatorze
fifteen	quinze
sixteen	seize
seventeen	dix-sept
eighteen	dix-huit
nineteen	dix-neuf
twenty	vingt
twenty one	vingt-et-un(e)
thirty	trente
forty	quarante
fifty	cinquante
sixty	soixante
seventy	soixante-dix
eighty	quatre-vingts
ninety	quatre-vingt-dix
one hundred	cent

German

The German language comprises two main dialects, High German (including standard literary German) and Low German. Standard German is an official language of Germany, Austria, Liechtenstein, Belgium, Luxembourg and Switzerland. The United States became home to many German immigrants in the 1800s; at one time, Congress was considering whether to make German an official language of the country. Within the European Union, German is the language with the most native speakers, more than English, French, Spanish and Italian. German is spoken by 38 million people in 38 countries.

Vowels

Vowels are usually pronounced long if followed by a consonant or by an h. However, if it is before st there is no rule.
In addition, the accent is usually on the first syllable with the exception of common prefixes such as b, ge,er,ent,emp,zer, and ver.

Diphthongs (two vowels together)

au	'ow' in cow
Au/Eu	'oy' in toy
Ei	'eye'
ie	'ee"

Consonants

Most of the consonants have the same sound in English. All consonants ending a word or syllable are voiceless. The **r** in German is usually spoken gutturally, especially at the beginning and end of words.

b	p	**st, sp**	st, sp, schp, scht
d	t	**w**	v
g	k (ich)	**v**	f
s	s and z	**sch**	sh
ß	ss	**ch, ig**	after the vowels, e, i, u and before r vowels a, o, and u
z	ts	**ng**	ng (never the ng-g)

Phrases for school

How are you?	Wie geht's dir?
Did you finish your homework?	Hast du deine Hausaufgaben gemacht?
What tests do you have today?	Welche Verhor hast du heute?
Welcome.	Willkommen.
Nice to meet you.	Es freut mıch, dich kennenzulernen.

Welcome to our school. . . . . Willkommen in unserer Schule.

My name is _____. . . . . Ich heiße _____.

What is your name? . . . . Wie heiße du?

Do you understand the teacher?. . . . . Verstehst du den Lehrer? Verstehst du die Lehrerin?

You need to turn in your homework everyday. . . . . Du musst jeden Tag deine Hausaufgaben machen.

Do you have any questions? . . . . Hast du irgendwelche Fragen?

Where are you from? . . . . Woher kommst du?

Do you have any brothers or sisters? . . . . Hast du Brüder oder Schwestern?

How are you adjusting to our school?. . . . . Wie kommst du in unserer Schule zurecht?

Do you speak English?. . . . . Sprechen sie Englisch?

Do you play any sports? . . . . Übst du einen Sport aus?

Do you have a girlfriend/boyfriend? . . . . Hast du eine Freundin? Hast du eine Freund?

What is your favorite subject in school? . . . . Was ist dein Lieblingsfach in der Schule?

What is your worst subject in school?. . . . . Welches Fach magst du gar nicht in der Schule?

Where is your homework? . . . . Wo sind deine Hausaufgaben?

Don't be late to class! . . . . Komm' nicht zu spät zum Klasse!

Please study tonight! . . . . Bitte lerne heute abend!

What test are you taking? . . . . Welche Arbeit schreibst du?

Do you need help? . . . . Brauchst du Hilfe?

May I help you?. . . . . Kann ich dir helfen?

Please pay attention. . . . . Bitte pass auf!

Good work! . . . . Gut gemacht!

Do you understand the test?. . . . . Verstehst du die Verhor?

Do you understand your homework?. . . . . Verstehst du deine Hausaufgaben?

I am proud of you. . . . . Ich bin stolz auf dich.

Keep up the good work! . . . . Mach weiter so!

Do you know where your next class is? . . . . Weißt du, wo deine nächste Klasse ist?

How was art class?. . . . . Wie war der Kunstkurs?

How was gym class? . . . . Wie war die Sportstunde? Wie war der Sportkurs?

How was music class? . . . . Wie war die Musikstunde? Wie war der Musikkurs?

Quiet please! . . . . Sei bitte leise! Sei bitte ruhig!

Please don't interrupt! . . . . Bitte unterbrich nicht!

Happy Birthday! . . . . Herzlichen Glückwunsch zum Geburtstag!

Common words and phrases

Hello . . . . Guten Tag

Goodbye. . . . . Auf Wiedersehen

Please. . . . . Bitte

Excuse me. . . . . Entschuldigen Sie

Thank you . . . . Danke

You're welcome . . . . Bitte schön

Nice to meet you.. . . . . Sehr erfreut. Freut mich (Sie kennen zu lernen.)

Good morning . . . . Guten Morgen

Good afternoon . . . . Guten Tag

Good evening. . . . . Guten Abend

Good night . . . . Gute Nacht

Yes . . . . Ja

No . . . . Nein
Maybe . . . . Vielleicht
Open . . . . Auf, offen
Closed . . . . Geschlossen
All . . . . Alles
A little . . . . Wenig, ein biBchen
A lot . . . . Sehr viel
Good . . . . Gut
Bad . . . . Schlecht

Questions

Who? . . . . Wer?
What? . . . . Was?
When? . . . . Wann?
Where? . . . . Wo?
Why? . . . . Warum?
How? . . . . Wie?
How much? . . . . Wieviel?
Where is _____? . . . . Wo ist _____?
What is this? . . . . Was ist das?
I do not understand.. . . . . Ich verstehe nicht
How do you say this in English? . . . . Wie heiBt das auf?
Do you speak English? . . . . Sprechen Sie Englisch?
What is your name? . . . . Wie heiBen Sie?
How are you? . . . . Wie gehts?
How much does this cost? . . . . Wieviel kostet das?
I will buy it. . . . . Ich nehme es.
I would like to buy _____. Ich mochte _____ kaufen.
Do you have _____? . . . . Haben Sie _____?
Do you accept credit cards? . . . . Akzeptieren Sie Kreditkarten? Nehmen Sie Kreditkarten?
What time is it? . . . . Wie spät ist es?

Where

Where's the bathroom? Where is the toilet? . . . . . . Wo ist die Toilette?
Where is _____? . . . . Wo ist _____?
Airport . . . . der Flughafen
Train station . . . . der Bahnhof
Bus station . . . . der Busbahnhof
Subway station . . . . der U-Bahnhof
Car rental agency . . . . die Autovermietung
Hotel . . . . das Hotel
Post office . . . . die Post
Bank . . . . die Bank
Police station . . . . die Polizeiwache, das Polizeirevier
Hospital . . . . das Krankenhaus
Pharmacy . . . . die Apotheke
Store, Shop . . . . das Geschäft

Restaurant .Gaststatte, das Restaurant
School . . . . .die Schule
Church . . . . .die Kirche
Restrooms .das WC, die Toilette
Left . . . . .Links
Right . . . . .Rechts
Near . . . . .Nahe
Far . . . . .Weit

Who
Mother . . . . .die Mutter
Father . . . . .der Vater
Brother . . . . .derBruder
Sister . . . . .die Schwester
Family . . . . .die Familie
Wife . . . . .die Frau
Husband . . . . .der Ehemana
Daughter . . . . .die Tochter
Son . . . . .der Sohn
Friend . . . . .der Freund (M), dieFreundin (F)
Teacher . . . . .der Lehrer, die Lehrerin
Student . . . . .der Student
Doctor . . . . .der Doktor
Policeman .der Polizist
Waiter, waitress . . . . .der Kellner, die Kellnerin

I . . . . .Ich
We . . . . .Wir
You (singular) . . . . .Du, Sie
You (plural) . . . . .Ihr
They . . . . .Sie

What
Train . . . . .die Bahn, der Zug
Bus . . . . .der Bus
Room . . . . .das Zimmer
Reservation . . . . .die Reservierung, Reserviert
Passport . . . . .der ReisepaB
Ticket . . . . .die Fahrkarte
Tourist information . . . . .das Fremdenverkehrsbuero, die Auskunftsstelle
Map . . . . .die Karte, die Landkarte
Postcard . . . . .die Postkarte
Stamps . . . . .die Briefmarke, Briefmarken
May I see a menu? . . . . .Kann ich ein Menu sehen?
I would like to order. . . . . .Ich mochte anordnen.
Please bring the check. . . . . .Die Rechnung, bitte. Zahlen, bitte.
Breakfast . . . . .das Frühstuck

Lunch . . . . das Mittagessen
Dinner . . . . das Abendessen
Bread . . . . das Brot
Coffee . . . . der Kaffee
Tea . . . . der Tee
Juice . . . . der Saft
Water . . . . das Wasser
Beer . . . . das Bier
Wine . . . . der Wein
Bread . . . . das Brot
Fruit . . . . die Frucht, das Obst
Salad . . . . der Salat
Beef . . . . das Rindfleisch
Pork . . . . das Schweinefleisch
Fish . . . . der Fisch
Chicken . . . . der Huhn
Vegetable . . . . das Gemuse

When

Today . . . . Heute
Yesterday . . . . Gestern
Tomorrow . . . . Morgen
Now . . . . Jetzt
Minute . . . . die Minute
Hour . . . . die Stunde
Arrive . . . . Ankommt
Depart . . . . Abfahrt
Day . . . . der Tag
Week . . . . die Woche
Month . . . . der Monat
Year . . . . das Jahr

Monday . . . . Montag
Tuesday . . . . Dienstag
Wednesday . . . . Mittwoch
Thursday . . . . Donnerstag
Friday . . . . Freitag
Saturday . . . . Samstag
Sunday . . . . Sonntag

January . . . . Januar
February . . . . Februar
March . . . . Marz
April . . . . April
May . . . . Mai
May . . . . Mai
June . . . . Juni

July . . . . Juli
August . . . . August
September . . . . September
October . . . . Oktober
November . . . . November
December . . . . Dezember

Fall . . . . der Herbst
Winter . . . . der Winter
Spring . . . . der Fruhling
Summer . . . . der Sommer

How many

zero . . . . Null
one . . . . Eins (ein,eine)
two . . . . Zwei
three . . . . Drei
four . . . . Vier
five . . . . Fünf
six . . . . Sechs
seven . . . . Sieben
eight . . . . Acht
nine . . . . Neun
ten . . . . Zehn

eleven . . . . Elf
twelve . . . . Zwölf
thirteen . . . . Dreizehn
fourteen . . . . Vierzehn
fifteen . . . . Fünfzehn
sixteen . . . . Sechzehn
seventeen . . . . Siebzehn
eighteen . . . . Achtzehn
nineteen . . . . Neunzehn
twenty . . . . Zwanzig

twenty one . . . . Einundzwanzig
thirty . . . . DreiBig
forty . . . . Vierzig
fifty . . . . Funfzig
sixty . . . . Sechzig
seventy . . . . Siebzig
eighty . . . . Achtzig
ninety . . . . Neunzig
one hundred . . . . Hundert

Gujarati

Gujarati is the official language of Gujarat, a state of India located on the western coast. Gujarati is spoken in Pakistan, Bangladesh, Nepal, South Africa and other countries with a large Gujarati population. The language is similar to Sanskrit, the ancient classical language of India and Hindu texts. It has 46 million speakers.

Vowels

Simple vowels

Vowel	Phonetic Description
i	close, front
u	close, back
e	close-mid, front
o	close-mid, back
E	open-mid, front
a	open, front

Consonants

Consonants	Phonetic Description
k	voiceless, touching the soft palate with the tongue, stop
kH	voiceless, aspirated, touching the soft palate with the tongue, stop
g	voiced, touching the soft palate with the tongue, stop
gH	voiced, aspirated, touching the soft palate with the tongue, stop
c	voiceless, tongue touch hard palate, stop
cH	voiceless, aspirated, tongue touch hard palate, stop
j	voiced, tongue touch hard palate, stop
jH	voiced, aspirated, tongue touch hard palate, stop
ÿ	voiceless, tip of tongue curled backwards, stop
ÿH	voiceless, aspirated, tip of tongue curled backwards, stop

ê	voiced, tip of tongue curled backwards, stop
êH	voiced, aspirated, tip of tongue curled backwards, stop
t	voiceless, touching upper front teeth, stop
tH	voiceless, aspirated, touching upper front teeth, stop
d	voiced, touching upper front teeth, stop
dH	voiced, aspirated, touching upper front teeth, stop
n	touching upper front teeth, nasal
p	voiceless, lips close together or touching, stop
pH	voiceless, aspirated, lips close together or touching, stop
b	voiced, lips close together or touching, stop
bH	voiced, aspirated, lips close together or touching, stop
m	lips close together or touching, nasal
y	tongue touch hard palate, semivowel
r	flap, touch ridge behind upper front teeth
l	breath passes on either or both sides of tongue, touch ridge behind upper front teeth
w	using one or both lips on surface of the tooth facing the lips, semivowel
s	voiceless, forcing breath through vocal tract, touch ridge behind upper front teeth
S	voiced, forcing breath through vocal tract, touch ridge behind upper front teeth
h	voiceless, forcing breath through vocal tract, glottal
ñ	breath passes on either or both sides of tongue, tip of tongue curled backwards

Phrases for school

How are you? . . . Kem chho?

Did you finish your homework? . . . Tame tamaaru homework puru karyu?

What tests do you have today? . . . Aaje taari kai pareeksha che?

Welcome. . . . Bhale padharo.

Nice to meet you.. . . Tamne mali ne ghano anand thayo.

Welcome to our school. . . . Amaari school maa tamaaro swaagat kariye chiye.

My name is _____. . . . Maaru naam _____ chhe.

What is your name? . . . Tamaaru naam su che?

Do you understand the teacher? . . . Tame shikshak ne samjhi shaki chho?

You need to turn in your homework everyday. . . . Tamaaru gharkaam dar roj aapwu jaroori chhe.

Do you have any questions? . . . Tamne koi prashna che?

Where are you from? . . . Tame kya thi cho?

Do you have any brothers or sisters? . . . Tamaara koi bhai athwa ben che?

How are you adjusting to our school? . . . Tame tamari shala ma kewi reete anukul thauchho?

Do you speak English? . . . Tame English boli shako cho?

Do you play any sports? . . . Tame koi ramat ramo cho?

Do you have a girlfriend/boyfriend? . . . Tamaare koi benpani athwaa mitr che?

What is your favorite subject in school? . . . School maa tamaaro man pasand vishay kayo che?

What is your worst subject in school? . . . School maa tamne kayo vishay nathi gamto?

Where is your homework? . . . Tamaaru ghar kaam kya che?

Don't be late to class! . . . Tamaari class/varg maa moraa na parso!

Please study tonight. . . . Maharbani kari ne raate bhanjo.

What test are you taking?. . . . . Tame kayi pariksha lai rahya chho?

Do you need help?. . . . . Tamne madad joiye che?

May I help you?. . . . . Hu tamne shu madad kari shaku chu?

Please pay attention.   . . . . Maharbani kari ne dhyaan aapo.

Good work!. . . . . Saras kaam!

Do you understand the test?. . . . . Tamne pareeksha maa samajh padi?

Do you understand your homework?. . . . . Tamne tamaaru grihakarya ma samajh pari

I am proud of you. Mane tamaara upar garv che.

Keep up the good work. . . . . Saras Kaam karta rehjo.

Do you know where your next class is?. . . . . . .Tamne khabar che ke tamaaru aana pachhi beejo class kya che?

How was art class?. Art Class kevo hato?

How was gym class?. . . . . Vyaayaam no varg kevo hato?

How was music class?. . . . . Sangit no varg kevo gayo?

Quiet please. . . . . Kripa kari ne shaanti rakho.

Please don't interrupt. . . . . Krupa kari ne vachche naa bolo.

You need to write a descriptive essay. . . . . Tamaare ek varnaveene nibandh lakhwaanu chhe.

You need to write a poem. . . . . Tamaare kavita lakhwani che.

The test is _____ . . . . Pariksha. chhe _____.

There is no school tomorrow. . . . . Kaale school nathi.

Happy Birthday!. . . . . Janam Din ni vadhaai!

Where are you going?. . . . . Tame kya jao cho ?

Where do you live?. Tame kya raho cho ?

Common words and phrases

Hello. . . . . Kem-cho.

Goodby. . . . . Aavjo.

Please . . . . krupa-kareene.

Excuse me . . . . Maaf karjo.

Thank you . . . . Aabhaar/Dhanyavaad.

You're welcome. . . . . tamaro swaagat chhe.

Nice to meet you. . . . . Tamaare maline aanand thayo.

Good morning. . . . . shubh prabhaat

Good afternoon. . . . . shubh madhyan

Good evening . . . . shubh saandhya

Good night. . . . . shubh raatri

Yes. . . . . haa

No. . . . . naa

Open. . . . . khullee (f), khullo (m), khullu (n)

Closed. . . . . bandh

All. . . . . badhu (n), badho (m), badhee (f)

A little. . . . . jaraa/thoru

A lot . . . . ghani/ghanu

Good. . . . . saaru/saras

Bad . . . . saaru nathi/kharaab

Questions

What?	Su/shu?
Where?	Kyaa?
How?	Kevi reete?
Where is _____?	Kyaa che?
What is this?	Aa shu chhe?
I do not understand..	Hu Samjhiyo nathi/Hu Samjhi nathi
How do you say this in English?	Aa angreji maa kevi reete kehsho?
Do you speak English?	Tame angreji bolo chho?
What is your name?	Tamaaru naam shu che?
How are you?	Tame kem chho?
How much does this cost?	Aani Keemmat ketlee che?
I will buy it.	Hu Aa Khareedi laish
I would like to buy _____	Maare khareedvu gumshe.
Do you have _____?	Tamaara paase che?
Do you accept credit cards?	Credit card sveekaaro/lau chho?
What time is it?	ketlaa vaagyaa che?

Where

Where's the bathroom? Where is the toilet?	Bathroom kyaa chhe?
Where is _____?	Kyaa aavyu?
Airport	airport/Hawaii addo
Train station	train station
Bus station	esti stand/bus station
Subway station	subway station
Car rental agency	kaar bhaade aapti agensi
Hotel	hotel
Post office	post office/Daak Ghar
Bank	bank
Police station	police chowki
Hospital	hospital/dawaa khaanu
Drug store/Pharmacy	davaani dukaan
Grocery store/store	storr/Kiraana ni dukaan
Restaurant	restoraan/hotal
School	skool
Church	charch/girijaaghar
Restrooms	bathroom
Left	daabi (baaju)
Right	jamni (baaju)
Far	door
Near	najik/Paase

Who

Mother	maa, maataa
Father	pita, baapuji
Husband	pati
Wife	patni
Son	putra, dikaro
Daughter	putri, dikri
Friend	mitra/benpani
I	hu, mane
We	ame, aapne
You (singular)	tu, tame
You (plural)	tame badha
They	teo

What

Train	train/rel gaadi
Bus	bas
Room	kamro, room/ordo
Reservation	anaamat, rizarveshan
Passport	paasport
Ticket	tikit
Map	naksho
Tourist information	yaatri maate maahiti
Postcard	post card
Stamps	tikit
Please bring the check.	Krupya kari ne bill laavo
Breakfast	nasto
Lunch	bapor nu bhojan
Dinner	raatri nu bhojan
Coffee	koaffee
Tea	chaa
Milk	dudh
Juice	ras
Water	paani
Bread	bred/pau
Fruit()fur	phal
Salad	salaad
Beef	beef
Pork	pork
Fish	maachli
Vegetable	shaak
Dessert	mithai
Salt	meethu
Pepper	mari
Beer	beer
Wine	daaru, waain

When

Today	aaj, aaje
Yesterday	gai kaal
Tomorrow	aavtii kaal
Depart	vidaai levi
Arrive	aavi pahochwu
Day	divas/din
Week	athvaadiyu/saptaah
Month	maas/mahino
Year	varsh
Monday	somvaar
Tuesday	mangalvaar
Wednesday	budhvaar
Thursday	guruvaar
Friday	shukravaar
Saturday	shanivaar
Sunday	ravivaar
January	jaanuaari
February	februaari
March	maarch
April	april
May	me
June	june
July	julaai
August	Ogast
September	Saptembar
October	Octobar
November	Navambar
December	Disembar
Fall	paankhar
Winter	shiyaaro
Spring	vasant (Rutu)
Summer	unaalo, greeshma (Rutu)

How Many

zero	shoonya
one	ek
two	be
three	tran
four	chaar
five	paaNch
six	cho
seven	saat
eight	aath
nine	nav
ten	dash, das
eleven	agiyaar
twelve	baar
thirteen	ter
fourteen	chaud
fifteen	pandar
sixteen	soL
seventeen	sattar
eighteen	adhaar
nineteen	ognees
twenty	vees
twenty one	ekvees
thirty	trees
forty	chaalees
fifty	pachaas
sixty	saahit
seventy	sittair
eighty	ehshee
ninety	nevu
one hundred	so

Hindi

Hindi is a phonetic language; it is spoken as it is written. Although related to the ancient Sanskrit language, Hindi has been strongly influenced by Farsi, Arabic, Portuguese and English. Hindi is the literary and official language of India; more than 180 million people in India regard Hindi as their mother tongue, and another 300 million use it as a second language.

Pronunciation

Long vowels	are aa, ah, as, ee, ii, oo, uu.
Short vowels a, i, u	as in the English word but, sit, book.
ai	the sound is short like in mat; au is like the 'o' in hot.
a~,e~, i~, o~, u~	nasalised
t and d	pronounced with the tongue curled back against the roof of the mouth

Nouns

Nouns have two genders, masculine and feminine. The nouns also change their position in a sentence.

Adjectives

Adjectives ending in aa agree in gender and number with their nouns.
However, in all cases, feminine is ii, and masculin (singular, plural) is (aa, e) and (e, e)

Phrases for school

How are you?	Aap kaise ho?
Did you finish your homework?	Aap ne apna ghar kaam pura kiya?
What tests do you have today?	Aaj aap ki kon si Pariksha hai?
Welcome.	Swaagat.
Nice to meet you.	Aap se milke khushi huyi.
Welcome to our school.	Hamaari paathshala me aapka swaagat hai.
My name is _____.	Mera naam _____ hai.
What is your name?	Aap ka naam kya hai?
Do you understand the teacher?	Aap apne shikshak ki baat samajhte ho?
You need to turn in your homework everyday.	Aap ko har roz aapkaa ghar ka kaam denaa chaahiye.
Where are you from?	Aap kis jagah se ho?
Do you have any brothers or sisters?	Aap ke bhai ya bahan hai?

How are you adjusting to our school? . . . . Aap apni pathshaala me apne aapko ko kaise samadhaan karte (M)/karti ho (F)?

Do you speak English? . . . . Kya Aap Angrezi bolte ho?

Do you play any sports? . . . . Kya Aap koi khel khelte ho?

Do you have a girlfriend/boyfriend? . . . . Kya Aap ka koi dost ya saheli hai?

What is your favorite subject in school? . . . . Aap ko kaun sa vishai pasand hai?

What is your worst subject in school? . . . . Aapko kaun sa visha pasand nahi hai?

Where is your homework? . . . . Aap ka ghar ka kaam kahan hai?

Don't be late to class! . . . . Aap kaksha mein der say mat janaa!

Please study tonight. . . . . Kripa karke aaj raat ko parna.

What test are you taking? . . . . Aap kon si pareeksha le rahe ho?

Do you need help? . . . . Aap ko madad chaahiye?

May I help you? . . . . Mein aapki kya sahayta kar sakta (M) /sakti (F) hoo?

Please pay attention.. . . . . Maherbaani karke dhyan deejiye.

Good work! . . . . Aacha kaam!

Do you understand the test? . . . . Aap ko pareeksha samajh me aa rahi hai?

Do you understand your homework? . . . . Aap ko ghar ka kaam samaj mein aata hai?

I am proud of you. . . . . Mujhe aap par garv hai.

Keep up the good work. . . . . Isi tarah apna kaam achchi tarah karte rehna.

Do you know where your next class is? . . . . Aap ko maalum hai aapki doosri kaksha kaha hai?

How was art class? . . . . Aapki chitra ki kaksha kaisi tthi?

How was gym class? . . . . Aapki gym ki kaksha kaisi tthi?

How was music class? . . . . Aapki sangeet ki kaksha kaisi tthi?

Quiet please. . . . . Kripa karke shaant rahe.

Please don't interrupt. . . . . Kripya karke avrodh na kare/kripya dakhal na de.

You need to write a poem. . . . . Aapko ek kavita likhni paregi.

There is no school tomorrow. . . . . Kal paathshaala ki chuththi hai.

Happy Birthday! . . . . Janmadin mubaarak ho!

Where are you going? . . . . Aap kahan jaa rahe ho?

Where do you live? . . . . Aapa kahan rehte ho?

Common words and phrases

Hello . . . . Namaste.

Goodbye . . . . Alvida (namaste)

Please . . . . Kripyaa

Excuse me . . . . Shama kare.

Thank you . . . . Dhanyavaad.

You're welcome . . . . Aapkaa svaagat hai.

Nice to meet you. . . . . Aapse milkar khushi huyi.

Good morning . . . . Shubha prabhaat.

Good afternoon . . . . Namaste.

Good evening . . . . Namaste.

Good night . . . . Shubha raatri.

Yes . . . . Ha

No . . . . Nahi

Open . . . . Khuli hai

Closed . . . . Band hai

All . . . . Sab (saaraa)

A little . . . . Chhoti

A lot . . . . Zyaada

Good . . . . Achchha

Bad . . . . Buraa

Questions

Who?	Kaun?
What?	Kya?
When?	Kab?
Where?	Kahan?
How?	Kaise?
How many?	Kitne?
Where is _____?	Kahan hai?
What is this?	Yah kyaa hai?
I do not understand..	Mujhe samajh me nahi aata...
How do you say this in English?	Aap ise angrezi mei kaise bolengay?
Do you speak English?	Kyaa aap angrezi bolte hain?
What is your name?	Aapka naam kya hai?
How are you?	Aap kaise (M)/kaisi (F) hai?
How much does this cost?	Iski keemat kyaa hai?
I will buy it.	Mai isko khareedunga (M)/khareedungi (F).
I would like to buy _____	Mai _____ khariidnaa chaahunga (M) /chaahungi (F).
Do you have _____?	Kya aapke paas _____ hai?
Do you accept credit cards?	Kya aap credit card sweekaarte hai?
What time is it?	Kyaa samay huaa hai?

Where

Where's the bathroom? Where is the toilet?	Aapkaa snanghar (sauchalay) kahan hai?
Where is _____?	Kahaan hai?
Airport	Havaai adda
Train station	Railway station
Bus station	Bus depot
Subway station.	Bhoomigat railway station
Car rental agency	kiraaye par gaadi dene ki dukaan
Hotel	Hotel
Post office	Daak ghar
Bank	Bank
Police station	Police station
Hospital	Haspataal
Drug Store/Pharmacy	Davaakhaanaa/Davaai ke dookaan
Grocery store/store	Store, dukan/modi ki dukaan/kirane ki dukaan
Restaurant	Restaurant (bhojnalay)
School	School, paathshaala
Church	Girjaaghar
Restrooms	Shauchalay
Left	Bayen
Right	Daayen
Far	Door
Near	Paas

Who

Mother	Mataji/maa
Father	Pitaji/baap
Brother	Bhai
Sister	Bahan
Family	Parivaar
Husband	Pati
Wife	Patni
Son	Beta
Daughter	Beti
Friend	Dost, mitra

I	Mai
We	Hum
You (singular)	Tum, aap
You (plural)	Aap sab
They	Vo sab

What

Train	rail
Bus	bus
Passport	passport
Ticket	ticket
Map	nakshaa
Tourist information	paryatan soochanaa
Please bring the check	kripaa raseed laaiye
Breakfast	naashtaa
Lunch	dopahar kaa khaanaa
Dinner	raat kaa khaanaa
Coffee	coffee
Tea	chai
Milk	doodh
Juice	ras
Water	paani
Bread	roti
Fruit	fal
Salad	salaad
Beef	gaay kaa maas
Pork	suwar kaa maas
Fish	machali
Chicken	murgi
Vegetable	sabzi
Dessert	mithaai
Salt	namak
Pepper	mirch
Beer	beer
Wine	wine

When

Today	aaj
Yesterday	kale
Tomorrow	kal
Arrive	aagman
Depart	prasthaan
Day	din
Week	hafta/saptaah
Month	maheena
Year	varsh
Monday	somavaar
Tuesday	mangalavaar
Wednesday	budhavaar
Thursday	brihaspativar
Friday	shukravar
Saturday	shanivaar
Sunday	ravivaar
January	Janwari
February	Farvari
March	March
April	Aprel
May	Mai
June	June
July	July
August	Agust
September	September
October	Uktoober
November	Novumber
December	Decumber
Fall	pathjhad
Winter	sardi/thundi
Spring	basant
Summer	garmi/greeshma

How many

zero	shunya
one	ek
two	do
three	teen
four	chaar
five	panch
six	chai
seven	saat
eight	aaththh
nine	nau
ten	dus
eleven	gyaaraha
twelve	baarah
thirteen	terah
fourteen	chaudah
fifteen	pandrah
sixteen	solah
seventeen	satrah
eighteen	aaThaaraha
nineteen	unnees
twenty	bees
twenty one	ikkees
thirty	tees
forty	chaalis
fifty	pachaas
sixty	saaTh
seventy	sattar
eighty	assee
ninety	nabbe
one hundred	eka sau

Hmong

Hmong classifies both a language and its native speakers; the Hmong minority lives mainly in Laos, Thailand, Burma, and Vietnam, and the related Miao minority resides in Southern China. The Hmong language is closely related to languages of Southeast Asia and Southern China and is often classified as a member of the Miao-Yao languages. Over a hundred thousand live in the United States. The Hmong language uses eight different tones, including a high tone, a high falling tone, a mid-rising tone, a mid tone, a breathy mid-low tone, a low tone, and low falling tone. The tone is indicated by the last letter of each word.

Pronunciation

a	'a' as in father	**au**	between the 'ou' of ouch and the 'ow' of throw.
ai	similar to "try"	**aw**	similar to 'oh'
e	as in they	**ee**	nasalized vowel between 'ing' and 'ung' in 'ring' and 'rung'
i	'e' as in "we"	**ia**	combined vowel of 'ee' and 'a' in see a man
o	'aw' in law or 'o' in lost	**oo**	nasalized vowel between 'do' followed by 'ng'
u	'o' in do or 'ou' in through	**ua**	sounds line combined vowel 'to a' said quickly
w	No English equivalent. Similar to Hmong 'i' and 'u' made with tongue close to the palate mid-way back in the mouth.		
ww	No English equivalent. Few words have this. Hmong 'w' with 'ng' following it.		
-n	nasalized vowel without ng in 'ee' and 'oo' "hon" sounds like 'aw' of law preceded by 'h'		

-h adding h after a consonant, means that the consonantis aspirated, meaning it is said with a puff of air, eg 'ph' sounds like the 'p' in 'part'

p	**ph**
t	**th**
d	**dh**
np	**nph**
tx	**txh**
ntx	**ntxh**

ch	like 'ch' in 'chew'	nch	like Hmong 'nc'
p	as in 'speak' without puff of air	np	'm' as in "comb"
npl	'm' blending into 'bl'	t	't' as in 'the'
nt	'n' blending into 'd'	tx	like 'ds'

ntx	'n' blending into Hmong 'tx'	d	like 'dream'
r	like a rolled Hmong 't'	nr	'n' blending into the Hmong 'r'
c	like 'ch' in 'chew'	nc	'n' blending into Hmong 'c'
ts	like 'j'	nts	'n; blending into Hmong 'ts'
k	unaspirated 'k'	nk	'n' blending into 'g' as in 'singer'
q, nq	like guttural 'k'	n, f, h	as in English
s	as 'sh' in 'sheep'	v, m, l,y	as in English
x	like 's' in 'seem'	z	like 'z' in 'azure'
g	like 'ng' in 'ping'	nl	'm' blending into an 'l' as the 'ml' in 'seemly'

Phrases for school

How are you? . . . . Koj nyob li cas?
Did you finish your homework? . . . . Koj puas tau ua koj cov ntawv qha mus ua tom tsev tiav?
What tests do you have today? . . . . Koj muaj tus xeem twg hnub no?
Welcome. . . . . Nyob zoo.
Nice to meet you. . . . . Zoo siab ntsib koj.
Welcome to our school. . . . . Zoo siab tos txais koj rau peb lub tsev kawm. ntawv.
My name is _____. . . . . Kuv lub npe hu ua _____.
What is your name? . . . . Koj lub npe hu li cas?
Do you understand the teacher? . . . . Koj puas to tau xibfwb?
You need to turn in your homework everyday. . . . . Koj yuav tsum xa koj cov homework tuaj txua hnub.
Do you have any questions? . . . . Koj puas muaj lus nug?
Where are you from? . . . . Koj tuaj qhov twg tuaj?
Do you have any brothers or sisters? . . . . Koj puas muaj nus los yog muam ?
How are you adjusting to our school? . . . . Peb lub tsev kawm ntawd xis koj npaum cas??
Do you speak English? . . . . Koj puas hais lus askiv?
Do you play any sports? . . . . Koj puas ua si sports li ?
Do you have a girlfriend/boyfriend? . . . . Koj puas muaj hluas nkauj/hluas nraug?
What is your favorite subject in school? . . . . Koj nyiam kawm dab tsi tshaj hauv tsev kawn ntawv
Where is your homework? . . . . Koj cov homework nyob qhov twg?
Don't be late to class! . . . . Tsis txob tuaj lig rau hauv chav kawm!
Please study tonight. . . . . Thov saib ntawv ib tsam.
What test are you taking? . . . . Koj yuav xeem tus xeem twg?
Do you need help? . . . . Koj puas xav tau kev pab?

May I help you? . . . . Kuv pab koj puas tau?
Please pay attention.. . . . . Thov mloog.
Good work! . . . . Zoo heev!
Do you understand the test? . . . . Koj puas to tau tus xeem?
Do you understand your homework? . . . . Koj puas to tau koj cov homework?
I am proud of you. . . . . Kuv zoo siab rau koj
Keep up the good work. . . . . Ua kom zoo li no twj ywm.
Do you know where your next class is? . . . . koj puas paub koj chav ntxiv mus nyob twg ?
How was art class? . . . . Koj chav kos duab nyob twg?
How was gym class? . . . . Koj chav gym zoo li cas?
How was music class? . . . . Koj chav kawm nkauj zoo li cas?
Quiet please. . . . . Thov ntsiag twj ywm.
Please don't interrupt. . . . . Tsis txob cuam tsuam.
You need to write a descriptive essay . . . . Koj yuav tau sau ib daim ntawv piav qhia.
You need to write a narrative essay. . . . . Koj yuav tau sau ib zaj dab neeg.
You need to write a comparison/contrast paper. . . . . Koj yuav tau sau ib daim ntawv txog kev sib piv.
Your paper is due _____ . . . . Tag sij hawm rau koj daim ntawv lawm.
There is no school tomorrow. . . . . Tsis muaj kawm ntawv tag kis.
The test is _____ . . . . Tus xeem yog _____.
Happy Birthday! . . . . Zoo siab hnub yug!

Common words and phrases
Hello . . . . Nyob zoo
Goodbye . . . . Sib ntsib dua
Please . . . . Thov
Excuse me . . . . Thov zam kev
Thank you . . . . Ua tsaug
You're welcome . . . . Tsis ua cas
Nice to meet you. . . . . Zoo siab ntsib koj
Good morning . . . . Nyob zoo sawv ntxov
Good afternoon . . . . Nyob zoo tav su dua?
Good evening . . . . Nyob zoo tsaus ntuj?
Good night . . . . Pw zoo
Yes . . . . yog
No . . . . tsis yog
Open . . . . qhib
Closed . . . . kaw
All . . . . tag nro
A little . . . . Mme
A lot . . . . loj
Good . . . . zoo
Bad . . . . phem

Questions
Who? . . . . Leej twg?
What? . . . . Dab tsi?
When? . . . . Thaum twg?
Where? . . . . Nyob qhov twg?
Why? . . . . Vim li cas
How? . . . . Ua li cas?
How many? . . . . Ntau npaum cas?
Where is _____? . . . . Nyob twg?
What is this? . . . . Nov yog dab tsi?
I do not understand.. . . . . Kuv tsis to taub.

How do you say this in English? . . . .Qhov no hais li cas lus Askiv?
Do you speak English? . . . . .Koj puas hais lus Askiv?
What is your name? . . . . .Koj lub npe hu li cas?
How are you? . . . . .Koj nyob li cas?
How much does this cost? . . . . .Qhov no rau nqi li cas?
I will buy it. . . . . .Kuv mam yuav qhov no.
I would like to buy _____ . . . . .Kuv xav yuav_____.
Do you have _____? . . . . .Koj puas muaj _____?
Do you accept credit cards? . . . . . . .Koj puas txais daim credit cards?
What time is it? . . . . .Tsawg teev lawm?

Where
Where's the bathroom? . . . . .Lub chav siv dej nyob twg ?
Airport . . . . .tshav dav hlau
Train station . . . . .tsev tsheb ciav hlau
Bus station . . . . .tsev tos tsheb ntiav loj
Car rental agency . . . . .chaw xauj tsheb
Hotel . . . . .tsev them nyiam so
Post office . . . . .tsev xa ntawv
Bank . . . . .txhab nyiaj
Police station . . . . .tsev tub ceev xwm
Hospital . . . . .tsev kho mob
Drug Store/Pharmacy . . . . .chaw muag tsuaj
Grocery store/store . . . . .khw
Restaurant . . . . .tsev noj mov
School . . . . .tsev kawm ntawv
Church . . . . .tsev teev ntuj
Restrooms . . . . .chav dej
Left . . . . .sab laug
Right . . . . .xab xis
Far . . . . .deb
Near . . . . .ze

Who
Mother . . . . .niam
Father . . . . .txiv
Brother . . . . .nus
Sister . . . . .muam
Family . . . . .tsev neeg
Husband . . . . .tus txiv
Wife . . . . .tus poj niam
Son . . . . .tub
Daughter . . . . .ntxhais
Friend . . . . .phooj ywg
Teacher . . . . .xibfwb
Student . . . . .menyuam kawm ntawv
Doctor . . . . .kws kho mob . . . .
Policeman . . . . .tub ceev xwm

I . . . . .kuv
We . . . . .peb
You (singular) . . . . .koj
You (plural) . . . . .koj
They . . . . .lawv

What

Train	tsheb ciav hlau
Bus	tsheb ntiav loj
Passport	daim passport
Ticket	daim pib
Map	ntawv qhia kev
Tourist information	tsev qhia txog kev mus ncig teb chaws
Please bring the check.	Thov nqa daim check.
Breakfast	tshais
Lunch	su
Dinner	hmo
Coffee	kas fes
Tea	tea
Milk	kua mis
Juice	kua txiv
Water	dej
Bread	qhaub cij
Fruit	txiv hmab txiv ntoo
Salad	zaub nyoos sib do
Beef	nqaij nyuj
Pork	nqaij npuav
Fish	ntsev
Chicken	qaib
Vegetable	zaub
Dessert	khoom noj txawm ncauj
Salt	ntsev
Pepper	hwj txob
Wine	cawv

When

Today	hnub no
Yesterday	hnag hmo
Tomorrow	tag kis
Arrive	txog
Depart	sawv kev
Now	tam sis no
Minute	ib feeb
Hour	ib teev
Day	hnub
Week	limtiam
Month	lub hli ntuj
Year	xyoo
Monday	Hnub ib
Tuesday	Hnub ob
Wednesday	Hnub peb
Thursday	Hnub plaub
Friday	Hnub tsib
Saturday	Hnub rau
Sunday	Hnub xya

August	Lub yim hli ntuj
September	Lub cuaj hli ntuj
October	Lub kaum hli ntuj
November	Lub kaum ib hli ntuj
December	lub kaum ob hli ntuj
Fall	Caij nplooj ntoo zeeg
Winter	Caij ntuj no
Spring	Caij nplooj ntoo hlav
Summer	Caij ntuj so

How many

zero	lub xoom
one	ib
two	ob
three	peb
four	plaub
five	tsib
six	rau
seven	xya
eight	yim
nine	cuaj
ten	kaum
eleven	kaum ib
twelve	kaum ob
thirteen	kaum peb
fourteen	kaum plaub
fifteen	kaum tsib
sixteen	kaum rau
seventeen	kaum xya
eighteen	kaum yim
nineteen	kaum cuaj
twenty	nees nkaum
twenty one	nees nkaum ib
thirty	peb caug
forty	plaub caug
fifty	tsib caug
sixty	rau caum
seventy	xya caum
eighty	yim caum
ninety	cuaj caum
one hundred	Ib puas

Italian

Italian is the direct successor of ancient Latin. It is the spoken native language in Italy, parts of Switzerland, San Marino, Sardinia and the former Yugoslavia. There are large immigrant communities in North and South America, North Africa and Australia.

Pronunciation

The Italian alphabet is similar to ours. The letters k, j, w, x, y occur only in foreign origin words.

gl	gli is pronounced as 'll' in Spanish.
Gn	gn has the same sound as the Spanish 'n'.
h	h is always silent and only occurs in groups with 'ch' and 'gh'.
a	pronounced as 'a' in bar.
e	pronounced like 'e' in sled or bed.
i	same as English 'i' long 'e' or 'ee' in bee.
o	pronounced like the 'o' in sold or log.
u	pronounced 'u' as in too or clue.
r	pronunced when the tip of the tongue is on the upper palate of the mouth.

Phrases for school

How are you? . . . . Como stai?
Did you finish your homework? . . . . Lei ha finito i suoi compiti?
What tests do you have today? . . . . Che esami hai oggi?
Welcome. . . . . Benvenuto.
Nice to meet you. . . . . Piacere di conoscerla.
Welcome to our school. . . . . Benvenuto alla nostra scuola.
My name is _____. . . . . Mi chiamo _____.
What is your name? . . . . Come ti chiami?
Do you understand the teacher? . . . . Lei capisce l'insegnante?
You need to turn in your homework everyday.. . . . . Lei ha bisogno di dare I compiti
di tutti I giorni.
Do you have any questions?. . . . . Lei ha qualche domande?

Where are you from? . . . . Da dove vieni?

Do you have any brothers or sisters? . . . . Qualche lei ha fratelli o qualche sorelle?

How are you adjusting to our school? . . . . Come ti senti alla nostra scuola?

Do you speak English?. . . . . Lei parla Inglese?

Do you play any sports? . . . . Practica qualche sport?

Do you have a girlfriend/boyfriend? . . . . Lei ha un'amica?

What is your favorite subject in school?. . . . . Qual'e il suo soggetto preferito nella scuola?

What is your worst subject in school?. . . . . Qual'e il suo soggetto peggiore nella scuola?

Where is your homework? . . . . Dove sono I compiti?

Don't be late to class! . . . . Non fare tardi alla classe!

Please study tonight. . . . . Per favore studia stasera.

What test are you taking? . . . . Quali esame stai facendo?

Do you need help? . . . . Lei ha bisognod' aiuto?

May I help you? . . . . La posso aiutare?

Please pay attention.. . . . . Per favore fa attenzione.

Good work! . . . . Buon Lavoro!

Do you understand the test?. . . . . Lei capisce il test?

Do you understand your homework?. . . . . Lei capisce il suoi compiti?

I am proud of you. . . . . Sono orgoglioso di lei.

Keep up the good work. . . . . Continua a fare buon lavoro.

Do you know where your next class is? . . . . Lei sa dove la prossima classe?

How was art class?. . . . . Come era la classe di arte?

How was gym class? . . . . Come era la classe di ginnastica?

How was music class? . . . . Come era la classe di musica?

Quiet please. . . . . Silenzio per favore.

Please don't interrupt. . . . . Per favore non interrompere.

You need to write a descriptive essay.. . . . . Lei ha bisogno di scrivere tema descrittiva.

You need to write a narrative essay. . . . . Lei ha bisogno di scrivere tema di narrazione.

You need to write a comparison/contrast paper. . . . . . . Lei ha bisogno di scrivere tema
di paragone/contrasto.

You need to write a poem. . . . . Lei ha bisogno di scrivere una poesia.

The homework is due _____ . . . . Il compiti e dovuto.

The test is _____ . . . . Il test e' _____.

Your project is due _____. . . . . Il suo progetto e dovuto.

Your paper is due _____ . . . . La sua tema e dovuta.

There is no school tomorrow. . . . . Non ci e' scuola domani.

Happy Birthday!. . . . . Buon compleanno!

Where are you going? . . . . Dove sta andando? Dove stai andando? Dove va?

Where do you live? . . . . Dove abiti? Dove abita?

Common words and phrases

Hello . . . . Salve, Ciao

Goodbye . . . . Arrivederci, Ciao

Please . . . . per favore

Excuse me . . . . mi scusi, scusa

Thank you . . . . Grazie.

You're welcome . . . . Prego.

Nice to meet you. . . . . Felice di conoscerla. Felice di conoscerti. Piacere.

Good morning . . . . buon giorno

Good afternoon . . . . buon pomeriggio

Good evening . . . . buona sera

Good night . . . . buona notte

Yes . . . . sì

No . . . . no

Maybe . . . . forse
Open . . . . aperto
Closed . . . . chiuso
All . . . . tutto, tutta, tutti, tutte
A little . . . . un poco, un pó, pochino
A lot . . . . molto, un sacco, moltissimo
Good . . . . buono (M), buona (F), bene
Bad . . . . cattivo (M), cattiva (F), male, non bene

Questions

Who? . . . . Chi?
What? . . . . Che?
When? . . . . Quando?
Where? . . . . Dove?
Why? . . . . Perche?
How? . . . . Come?
How much? . . . . Quanto?
Where is _____? . . . . Dove si trova?
What is this? . . . . Cosa e questo?
I do not understand.. . . . . Non capisco.
How do you say this in English? . . . . Come si dice questo in Inglese?
Do you speak English. . . . . Parla Inglese?
What is your name? . . . . Come si chiama? Come ti chiami?
How are you? . . . . Come sta? Come stai?
How much does this cost? . . . . Quanto costa?
I will buy it. . . . . Va bene, lo compro
I would like to buy _____. . . . . Mi piacerebbe comprare _____.
Do you have _____? . . . . Avreste _____?
Do you accept credit cards? . . . . Accettate carte di credito?
What time is it? . . . . Che ora e'?

Where

Where's the bathroom? Where is the toilet? . . . . . Dov' e' il bagno?
Where is _____? . . . . Dove si trova?
Airport . . . . aeroporto
Train station . . . . stazione (del treno)
Bus station . . . . stazione degli autobus
Subway Station . . . . stazione della metropolitana
Car rental agency . . . . autonoleggio
Hotel . . . . albergo, hotel
Post office . . . . ufficio postale, posta
Bank . . . . banca
Police station . . . . polizia, stazione di polizia
Hospital . . . . ospedale
Drug Store/Pharmacy . . . . farmacia
Grocery Store/store. . . . . negozio

Restaurant . . . . .ristorante
School . . . . .scuola
Church . . . . .chiesa
Restrooms . . . . .toilettes, bagni, servizi
Left . . . . .sinistra
Right . . . . .destra
Far . . . . .lontano
Near . . . . .vicino

Who
Mother . . . . .madre
Father . . . . .padre
Brother . . . . .fratello
Sister . . . . .sorella
Family . . . . .la famiglia
Husband . . . . .marito
Wife . . . . .moglie
Son . . . . .figlio
Daughter . . . . .figlia
Friend . . . . .amico (M), amica (F)
Teacher . . . . .maestro
Student . . . . .studente
Doctor . . . . .dottore
Policeman . . . . .poliziotto
Waiter . . . . .cameriere
I . . . . .io
We . . . . .noi
You (singular) . . . . .tu, lei
You (plural) . . . . .voi
They . . . . .essi (m)

What
Train . . . . .treno
Room . . . . .camera, stanza
Reservation . . . . .prenotazione
Passport . . . . .passaporto
Ticket . . . . .biglietto
Map . . . . .mappa, cartina geografica, cartina stradale
Tourist information . . . . .informazioni turistiche
Postcard . . . . .cartolina postale
Stamps . . . . .francobolli
May I see a menu? . . . . .Posso vedere un menu?
I would like to order. . . . . .Vorrei ordinare
Please bring the check. . . . . .Il conto, per favore.
Breakfast . . . . .prima colazione
Lunch . . . . .pranzo
Dinner . . . . .cena

Coffee . . . . caffe'
Tea . . . . te
Milk . . . . il latte
Juice . . . . succo
Water . . . . acqua
Bread . . . . pane
Fruit . . . . frutta
Salad . . . . insalata
Beef . . . . manzo
Pork . . . . maiale
Fish . . . . pesce
Chicken. . . . . il pollo
Vegetable . . . . legumi, verdura,
                                    ortaggio
Dessert . . . . dessert, dolce
Salt . . . . sale
Pepper . . . . pepe
Beer . . . . birra
Wine . . . . vino

When
Today . . . . oggi
Yesterday . . . . ieri
Tomorrow . . . . domani
Now . . . . adesso
Minute . . . . il minuto
Hour . . . . l'ora
Arrive . . . . arriva
Depart . . . . parte

Day . . . . il giorno
Week . . . . settimana
Month . . . . mese
Year . . . . anno

Monday . . . . lunedi
Tuesday . . . . martedi
Wednesday . . . . mercoledi
Thursday . . . . giovedi
Friday . . . . venerdi
Saturday . . . . sabato
Sunday . . . . domenica

January . . . . gennaio
February . . . . febbraio
March . . . . marzo
April . . . . aprile

May . . . . maggio
June . . . . giugno
July . . . . luglio
August . . . . agosto
September . . . . settembre
October . . . . ottobre
November . . . . novembre
December . . . . dicembre

Fall. . . . . autunno
Winter . . . . inverno
Spring . . . . primavera
Summer . . . . estate

How many
zero . . . . zero
one . . . . uno
two . . . . due
three . . . . tre
four . . . . quattro
five . . . . cinque
six . . . . sei
seven . . . . sette
eight . . . . otto
nine . . . . nove
ten . . . . dieci

eleven . . . . undici
twelve . . . . dodici
thirteen . . . . tredici
fourteen . . . . quattordici
fifteen . . . . quindici
sixteen . . . . sedici
seventeen . . . . diciassette
eighteen . . . . diciotto
nineteen . . . . diciannove
twenty . . . . venti

twenty one . . . . ventuno
thirty . . . . trenta
forty . . . . quaranta
fifty . . . . cinquanta
sixty . . . . sessanta
seventy . . . . settanta
eighty . . . . ottan
ninety . . . . novanta
one hundred . . . . cento

Japanese

Japanese is spoken throughout the nation of Japan. Japanese can also be found in emigrant communities in Australia, Brazil, Peru, and the United States, and it is spoken by over 120 million people. Interestingly, Japanese evolved three different writing styles: hiragana and katakana are phonetic scripts, while kanji, based on Chinese characters, is symbolic.

Vowels and Consonants

The Japanese language has a, e, i, o, and u. The consonants are h, k, m, n, y, r, w, and the nasal n. The vowels length distinguishes the word and the consonants in front of vowles a, o, and u.

Phrases for school

How are you? . . . . Genki desuka?

Did you finish your homework? . . . . Shyukudai wa owarimashitaka?

What tests do you have today? . . . . Kyou wa nanno tesuto ga arimasuka?

Welcome. . . . . You koso.

Nice to meet you. . . . . Yoroshiku.

Welcome to our school. . . . . .Watashitachino gakkou ni youkoso/Youkoso watashitachino gakko e.

My name is _____. . . . . Watashi no namae wa _____ desu.

What is your name? . . . . Anatano namae wa nandesuka?

Do you understand the teacher? . . . . Sono sensei no itteirukoto ga wakarimasuka?

You need to turn in your homework everyday.. . . . . Anata wa mainich shyukudai wo teishyutsu shinakutewa ikemasen.

Where are you from? . . . . Dokokara kitanodesuka?

Do you have any brothers or sisters? . . . . Kyoudai wa imasuka?

How are you adjusting to our school? . . . . Watashitachi no gakkou wa doudesuka?

Do you speak English?. . . . . Eigo wo hanasemasuka?

Do you play any sports? . . . . Nanika undou wo yattemasuka?

Do you have a girlfriend/boyfriend? . . . . Koibito wa imasuka?

What is your favorite subject in school?. . . . . Ichiban sukina kyouka wa nandesuka?

What is your worst subject in school?. . . . . Ichiban kiraina kyouka wa nandesuka?

Where is your homework? . . . . Shyukudai wa dokodesuka?

Don't be late to class! . . . . Jugyou ni okuretewa ikemasen!

Please study tonight. . . . . Konya wa benkyou wo shitekudasai.

What test are you taking?. Nanno tesuto wo uketeirunodesuka?

Do you need help?. . . . . Tasuke ga irimasuka? Herupu ga irimasuka?Herupu ga hitsu you desuka?/Herupu ga hitsu you desuka?

May I help you?. . . . . Tetsudai mashyouka?

Please pay attention. . . . . Chu moku moku shite kudasai.

Good work!. . . . . Yoku yatta! Yoku dekimashita.

Do you understand the test? . . . . Tesuto wo rikaidekimasuka?

Do you understand your homework? . . . . Shyukudai wo rikaidekimasuka?

I am proud of you.. . . . . Anata wo hokori ni omottemasu.

Keep up the good work. . . . . Korekaramo ganbare.

Do you know where your next class is? . . . . Tsugino class ga dokoka wakuru?

How was art class? . . . . Bijyutsu no kurasu wa doudesuka?

How was gym class?. . . . . Taiiku no kurasu wa doudesuka?

How was music class? . . . . Ongaku no kurasu wa doudesuka?

Quiet please. . . . . Shizukani shitekudasai.

Please don't interrupt. . . . . Jama wo shinaide kudasai.

You need to write a descriptive essay. . . . . Shouron wo kakinasai.

You need to write a narrative essay. . . . . Monogatari wo kakinasai.

You need to write a poem. Shi wo kakinasai.

The homework is due _____ . . . . Shyukudai no teishutsubi wa _____ desu.

The test is _____. . . . . Tesuto wa _____ desu.

Your project is due _____ . . . . Anata no purojekuto no teishutsubi wa _____ desu.

There is no school tomorrow. . . . . Ashita wa gakkou ga arimasen.

Where are you going? . . . . Dokoe ikunodesuka?

Where do you live? . . . . Dokoni sunde imasuka?

Happy Birthday! . . . . Tanjoubi omedetou!

Common words and phrases

Hello . . . . Konnichiwa.

Goodbye . . . . Sayounara.

Please . . . . Douzo, Onegai shimasu.

Excuse me . . . . Sumimasen, Shitsurei shimasu.

Thank you . . . . Arigato.

You're welcome . . . . Douitashimashite .

Nice to meet you. . . . . Oai dekite ureshii desu/Hajime mashite.

Good morning . . . . ohayou gozaimasu

Good afternoon . . . . Konnichiwa.

Good evening . . . . Konbanwa.

Good night . . . . Oyasuminasai.

Yes . . . . hai

No . . . . iie

Maybe . . . . osoraku/tabun

Open . . . . aku/akeru

Closed . . . . shimatteiru

All . . . . zenbu/subete

A little	sukoshi/chotto
A lot	takusan
Good	ii/yoi
Bad	warui/yokunai

Questions

Who?	Dare ga/Donata ga?/Dare
What?	Nan no?/nani?
When?	Itsu?
Where?	Doko (de/ni)?
Why?	Naze, Doshite?
How?	Doyatte?/Donoyouni?
How much?	Ikura?
Where is _____?	Wa doko desu ka?
What is this?	Korewa nan desuka?.
I do not understand..	Wakarimasen.
How do you say this in English?	Kore wa Eigo de nan to iimasuka?
Do you speak English?	Anata wa Eigo wo hanasemasuka?
What is your name?	Anata no namae wa nandesuka?
How are you?	Ogenki desu ka?
How much does this cost?	Korewa ikura desuka?
I will buy it.	Sore wo kaimasu.
I would like to buy ____.	Wo kaitai nodesu ____.
Do you have ____?	_____wa arimasuka/_____wo motteimasuka?
Do you accept credit cards?	Kurejiti to kaado de kaemasuka?
What time is it?	Nanji desuka?

Where

Where's the bathroom? Where is the toilet?	Toire wa doko desu ka?
Where is ____?	_____ wa doko desu ka?
Airport	kuukou/hikoujou
Train station	eki
Bus station	basu tei
Subway Station	chikatetsu no eki
Car rental agency	kuruma rentaru no dairiten
Hotel	hoteru
Post office	yuubinkyoku
Bank	ginkou
Police station	keisatsusho
Hospital	byouin
Drug store/pharmacy	yakkyoku
Grocery store/store	omise
Restaurant	resutoran/shokudou
School	gakkou
Church	kyoukai
Restrooms	toire

Left . . . . hidari
Right . . . . migi
Far . . . . tooku/tooi
Near . . . . chikaku/chikai

Who
Mother . . . . haha/okaasan/mama
Father . . . . chichi/otousan/papa
Brother . . . . kyodai/oniisan/otouto
Sister . . . . shimai/ane/oneesan/imouto
Family . . . . kazoku
Husband . . . . shujin, otto
Wife . . . . kanai, tsuma
Son . . . . musuko
Daughter . . . . musume
Friend . . . . tomodachi
Teacher . . . . sensei
Student . . . . gakusei/seito
Doctor . . . . isha
Policeman . . . . kei (satsu) kan
Waiter . . . . ueitaa
I . . . . watashi/watakushi/boku
We . . . . watashi tachi/boku tachi/wareware
You (singular) . . . . kimi, anata
You (plural) . . . . anatagata/anatatachi
They . . . . karera/knojotachi

What
Train . . . . kisha, ressha
Bus . . . . basu
Room . . . . heya
Reservation . . . . yoyaku
Passport . . . . pasupooto
Ticket . . . . chiketto
Map . . . . chizu
Tourist information . . . . (ryokou) annaisho
Postcard . . . . e hagaki
Stamps . . . . kitte
Please bring the check. . . . . okanjouwo onegai shimasu.
Breakfast . . . . choushoku
Lunch . . . . chuushoku
Dinner . . . . yuushoku
Coffee . . . . koohii
Tea . . . . ocha, koucha
Milk . . . . miruku/gyunyu
Juice . . . . juusu

Water . . . . mizu
Bread . . . . pan
Fruit . . . . kudamono
Salad . . . . sarada
Beef . . . . gyuu niku, biifu
Pork . . . . buta niku, pooku
Fish . . . . sakana
Chicken . . . . keiniku, chikin
Vegetable . . . . yasai
Dessert . . . . desaato
Salt . . . . shio
Pepper . . . . kosho
Beer . . . . biiru
Wine . . . . wain

When

Today . . . . kyouy
Yesterday . . . . kinou
Tomorrow . . . . asu, ashita
Now . . . . ima
Minute . . . . fun
Hour . . . . jikan
Arrive . . . . tsuku
Depart . . . . saru

Day . . . . hi/bi/nichi
Week . . . . shuu
Month . . . . tsuki
Year . . . . nen, toshi

Monday . . . . getsuyou bi
Tuesday . . . . kayou bi
Wednesday . . . . suiyou bi
Thursday . . . . mokuyou bi
Friday . . . . kinyou bi
Saturday . . . . doyou bi
Sunday . . . . nichiyou b

January . . . . ichi gatsu
February . . . . ni gatsu
March . . . . san gatsu
April . . . . shi gatsu
May . . . . go gatsu
June . . . . roku gatsu
July . . . . shichi gatsu

August . . . . hachi gatsu
September . . . . ku gatsu
October . . . . juu gatsu
November . . . . juu ichi gatsu
December . . . . juu ni gatsu

Fall . . . . aki
Winter . . . . fuyu
Spring . . . . haru
Summer . . . . natsu

How many

zero . . . . zero
one . . . . ichi
two . . . . ni
three . . . . san
four . . . . yon/shi
five . . . . go
six . . . . roku
seven . . . . nana/shichi
eight . . . . hachi
nine . . . . kyuu
ten . . . . juu

eleven . . . . juu ichi
twelve . . . . juu ni
thirteen . . . . juu san
fourteen . . . . juu yon(shi)
fifteen . . . . juu go
sixteen . . . . juu roku
seventeen . . . . juu nana
eighteen . . . . juu hachi
nineteen . . . . juu kyu
twenty . . . . ni juu

twenty one . . . . ni juu ichi
thirty . . . . san juu
forty . . . . yon juu
fifty . . . . go juu
sixty . . . . roku juu
seventy . . . . nana juu
eighty . . . . hachi juu
ninety . . . . kyuu juu
one hundred . . . . hyaku

Korean

Korean is the language spoken in North and South Korea. Korean culture has been influenced by the Mongols, Chinese and Japanese. While educated Koreans had used a system of Chinese characters called hanja for centuries, an easier, phonetic system called hangul was not developed until the fifteenth century. Korean is spoken by over 75 million people, of which 1.5 million live in the United States.

Consonants, Double consonants, Vowels

Korean consonants are pronounced much softer between two vowels in the middle of the word and double consonants are stopped consonants or a pause in breath when speaking. The Korean language has ten basic vowels but are generally spelled with an o as the initial consonant.

Phrases for school

How are you?	An-yeong ha-se-yo?
Did you finish your homework?	Sook-jae-reul ta hae-sseum-ni-kka?
What tests do you have today?	O-neul moo-seum shi-heom-eul bom-ni-kka?
Welcome.	Hwan-yeong ham-ni-da.
Nice to meet you.	Man-naso ban-gap-seum-ni--da.
Welcome to our school.	Oo-ri hag-yo-ay o-shin-geol hwan-yeong ham-ni-da.
My name is _____.	Chae irum-eun _____ im-ni-da.
What is your name?	I-rum-ee o-tto-kay doe-shi-n--eun jee-yo?
Do you understand the teacher?	Seon-saeng-nim mal-seum-ee ee-hae doe-shim-ni-kka?
You need to turn in your homework everyday.	Ma-il sook-jae-reul jae-cheul-hal pil-yo-ga i-sseum-ni-da.
Where are you from?	Chool-shinjee-neun o-dee-shim-ni-kka?
Do you have any questions?	Jil-mun-ee i-ssum-ni-kka?
Do you have any brothers or sisters?	Hyeong-jae-na ja-mae-ga i-sseum-ni-kka?
How are you adjusting to our school?	Oo-ri hag-yo-ay otto-kay jepk-eung ha-go i-sseum ni-kka?
Do you speak English?	Yong-o-ro mal-hal soo i-sseum-ni-kka?
Do you play any sports?	Oon-dong-eul ha-shim-ni-kka?
Do you have a girlfriend/boyfriend?	Yeo-ja chin-gu/nam-ja chin-gu-ga i-sseum-ni-kka?

What is your favorite subject in school? . . . . Hag-yo-eso jae-il jo-a-ha-neun gwa-mok-eun moo-eo-shim-ni-kka?

What is your worst subject in school? . . . . Hag--yo-eso ga-jang seong-jeok-ee ddo-ro-ji-neun gwa-mok-eun moo-eo-shim-ni-kka?

Where is your homework? . . . . Sook-jae-neun o-di-ay i-sseum-ni-kka?

Don't be late to class! . . . . Soo-eop-ay jee-gak-ha-ji ma-se-yo!

Please study tonight. . . . . O-neul-bam, gong-boo-ha-se-yo.

What test are you taking? . . . . Moo-seun shi-heom-eul bo-go i-sseum-ni-kka?

Do you need help? . . . . Do-oom-ee pi-ryo-ha-shim-ni-kka?

May I help you? . . . . Do-wa deu-ril-ka--yo?

Please pay attention. . . . . Joo-wee-reul gee-eul-yo joo-se-yo.

Good work! . . . . Jal hae-sseum-ni--da!

Do you understand the test? . . . . Shi-heom nae-yong-ee ee-hae-doem-ni-kka?

Do you understand your homework? . . . . Sook-jae nae-yong-ee ee--hae-doem-ni-kka?

I am proud of you. . . . . Dang-shin-ee ja-rang-seu-rop-seum-ni-da.

Keep up the good work. . . . . Gye-sok jal ha-se-yo.

Do you know where your next class is? . . . . Da-eum soo-eop-eun o-dee-eso ha-neun-jee a-shim-ni-kka?

How was art class? . . . . Mee-sool soo-eop-eun o-ttae-sseum-ni-kka?

How was gym class? . . . . Chae-yook soo-eop-eun o-ttae-ssum-ni-kka?

How was music class? . . . . Eu-mag soo-eop-eun o-ttae-ssum-ni-kka?

Quiet please. . . . . Jo-yong-hee ha-se-yo.

Please don't interrupt. . . . . Ggee-eo deuljee maseyo.

Happy Birthday! . . . . Saeng-il chook-ha ham-ni-da!

Where are you going? . . . . O-die ka-shim-ni-ka?

Where do you live? . . . . O-die sa-shim-ni-ka?

Common words and phrases

Hello. . . . . An-nyong ha-se-yo.

Goodbye. . . . . An-nyong-hi ka-ship-si-o.

Please. . . . . Pu-di, Che-bal

Excuse me. . . . . Che-song ham-ni--da.

Thank you. . . . . Kam-sa-ham-ni-da.

You're welcome. . . . . Chon-man-e mal-sum-im-ni-da

Nice to meet you. . . . . Man-na-so pan-kap-sum-ni-da

Good morning. . . . . An-nyong ha-shim-ni-ka

Good afternoon. . . . . An-nyong ha-shim-ni-ka

Good evening. . . . . An-nyong ha-shim-ni-ka

Good night. . . . . An-nyong-hi chu-mu-ship-sio

Yes . . . . ne

No . . . . a-nim-ni-da , a-ni-yo

Maybe . . . . a-ma

Open . . . . yong-up jung

Closed . . . . ma-gam

All . . . . modu

A little .... chokum
A lot .... mani
Good .... chosumnida
Bad .... shilsumnida

Questions

Who? .... Nu-ga?
What? .... Mu-?
When? .... On-je?
Where? .... O-ddi-so?
How? .... O-do-ke hae-so?
How much? .... Ul-ma ip-ni-gya?
Where is _____? .... _____ o-die i-sum-ni-ka ?
What is this? .... Igo-sun mu-wo-im-ni-ka?
I do not understand. .... Chal mo-ru-ge-sum-ni-da
How do you say this in English? .... Young-o-ro mu-wo-shim-ni-ka?
Do you speak English? .... Young-o-rul hal-jul a-shim-ni-ka?
What is your name? .... Tang-shin i-ru-mun mu-wo-shim-ni-ka?
How are you? .... O-toke chi-ne-go-ke-shim-ni-ka?
How much does this cost? .... Igo-sun Ol-ma-im-ni-ka?
I will buy it. .... Igo-sul sa-ge-sum-nida.
I would like to buy _____ .... _____ rul(ul) sa-go sip-sum-ni-da.
Do you have_____? .... _____ yi isum-nika?
Do you accept credit cards? .... Shin-yong card-rul pa-du-shim-ni-ka?
What time is it? .... Myot-shi-im-ni-ka?

Where

Where is _____? .... _____ o-die isum-ni-ka?
Airport .... kong-hang
Train station .... ki-cha-yok
Bus station .... bus chung-ko-jang
Subway station .... jon-chol-yok
Car rental agency .... ja-dong-cha te-yo-jom
Hotel .... ho-tel
Post office .... u-che-kuk
Bank .... un-heng
Police station .... kyung-chal-so
Hospital .... pyung-won
Drug Store/pharmacy .... yak-kuk
Grocery store/store .... ka-ge
Restaurant .... shik-dahng
School .... hak-gyo
Church .... kyo-he
Restrooms .... hwa-jang-sil

Left . . . . wen-chok, cha-chuk
Right . . . . orun-chok, u-chuk
Far . . . . mun
Near . . . . ga-ka-un

Who

Mother . . . . o-mo-ni
Father . . . . a-bo-ji
Brother . . . . hyong-nim
Sister . . . . nu-nim (older), nwi-tong-saeng (younger)
Family . . . . ga-jok
Husband . . . . nam-pyon
Wife . . . . a-ne, cho
Son . . . . a-dul
Daughter . . . . tal
Friend . . . . chin-gu
Teacher . . . . son-saeng-nim
Student . . . . hak-saeng
Doctor . . . . ui-sa
I . . . . na
We . . . . u-ri
You (singular) . . . . no, tang-shin
You (plural) . . . . tang-shin-dul
They . . . . ku-dul

What

Train . . . . ki-cha
Bus . . . . bus
Room . . . . bahng
Reservation . . . . ye-yak
Passport . . . . yok-kwon
Ticket . . . . pyo
Map . . . . ji-do
Tourist information . . . . kwan-kang-gag an-ne
Postcard . . . . yop-so
Stamps . . . . uu-pyo
Please bring the check. . . . . ke-san-so-rul chu-sip-sio
Breakfast . . . . a-chim
Lunch . . . . chom-shim
Dinner . . . . cho-nyok
Coffee . . . . ko-pyi, coffee
Tea . . . . cha
Milk . . . . u-yu
Juice . . . . ju-su, juice

Water . . . . mool
Bread . . . . pang
Fruit . . . . kwa-il
Salad . . . . sa-ra-da, salad
Beef . . . . so-ko-gi
Pork . . . . te-ji-ko-gi
Fish . . . . seng-son
Chicken. . . . . dak-ko-gi
Vegetable . . . . che-so
Dessert . . . . hu-sik
Salt . . . . so-gum
Pepper . . . . hu-chu
Beer . . . . mek-ju
Wine . . . . po-do-ju

When

Today . . . . o-nul
Yesterday . . . . o-je
Tomorrow . . . . ne-il
Now . . . . ji-kum
Minute . . . . il-bun
Hour . . . . si-gan
Arrive . . . . do-chak
Depart . . . . chul-bal

Day il
Week . . . . joo
Month . . . . wol
Year . . . . nyon

Monday . . . . wol-yo-il
Tuesday . . . . hwa-yo-il
Wednesday . . . . su-yo-il
Thursday . . . . mok-yo-il
Friday . . . . kum-yo-il
Saturday . . . . to-yo-il
Sunday . . . . il-yo-il

January . . . . il-wol
February . . . . yi-wol
March . . . . sam-wol
April . . . . sa-wol
May . . . . o-wol
June . . . . yu-wol

July . . . . chil-wol
August . . . . pal-wol
September . . . . ku-wol
October . . . . sip-wol
November . . . . sip-il-wol
December . . . . sip-yi-wol

Fall. . . . . ga-ul
Winter . . . . gyu-wool
Spring . . . . bohm
Summer . . . . yo-rum

How many

Zero . . . . yong, kong
one . . . . il/ha-na
two . . . . yi/dool
three . . . . sam/set
four . . . . sa/net
five . . . . o/da-sut
six . . . . yook/yu-sut
seven . . . . chil/il-goap
eight . . . . pal/yu-dul
nine . . . . ku/ah-hoap
ten . . . . sip/yul

eleven . . . . sip-il/yul-ha-na
twelve . . . . sip-yi/yul-dool
thirteen . . . . sip-sam/yul-set
fourteen . . . . sip-sa
fifteen . . . . sip-o
sixteen . . . . sip-yuk
seventeen . . . . sip-chil
eighteen . . . . sip-pal
nineteen . . . . sip-gu
twenty . . . . yi-sip

twenty one . . . . yi-sip-il
thirty . . . . sam-sip
forty . . . . sa-sip
sixty . . . . yuk-sip
seventy . . . . chil-sip
eighty . . . . pal-sip
ninety . . . . ku-sip
one hundred . . . . baek

Russian

Russian is the official language of Russia and is in common use in the former Soviet Union. Until the late 1900s, Russian was taught in all the Soviet Republics. It is a Slavic language that includes three groups of dialects. Developed by Cyrillic monks, the Russian alphabet is related to the Greek alphabet. The principal countries of usage include: Russia, United States, Canada, Israel, Azerbaijan, Belarus, Estonia, Georgia, Kazakhstan, Kyrghystan, Lithuania, Moldova, Latvia, Tajikistan, Turkmenistan, Ukraine, Uzbekistan, Germany, Norway, Poland, Mongolia, Bulgaria, China, Uruguay and Czech Republic.

Vowels

There are eight vowels in Russian: i, e, e, o, u, yu, a, ya. In unaccented position, e and o undergo reduction and are symbolized as i and a respectively.

Consonants

There are 36 consonants in Russian. Most consonants come in pairs, hard (non-palatalized) and soft (palatalized).

Phrases for school

How are you?	Kak ty? Kak dela?
Did you finish your homework?	Ty zakonchil svoyu damashnyuyu rabotu?
What tests do you have today?	Kakiye testy u tebya sevodnya?
Welcome.	Pazhaluysta; Dobro Pazhalovat'.
Nice to meet you.	Rad poznakomitsya s vami.
Welcome to our school.	Dobro pazhalovat' v nashu shkolu.
My name is _____.	Menya zavut _____.
What is your name?	Kak tebya zavut?
Do you understand the teacher?	Ty panimayesh uchitelya?
You need to turn in your homework everyday.	Tebe nuzhno zdavat damashnyuyu rabotu kazhdiy den.
Do you have any questions?	U tebya yest voprosy?
Where are you from?	Otkuda ty?
Do you have any brothers or sisters?	U tebya est bratiya ili syostry?
How are you adjusting to our school?	Kak ty privykayesh k nashey shkole?
Do you speak English?	Ty gavarish po angliyski?

Do you play any sports? . . . . Ty zanimayeshsya kakim-nibud' sportom?

Do you have a girlfriend/boyfriend? . . . . U tebya yest padruga/drug?

What is your favorite subject in school? . . . . Kakoy tvoy samiy lyubimiy predmet v shkole?

What is your worst subject in school? . . . . Kakoy predmet tebe ne nravitsya bolshe vsego?

Where is your homework? . . . . Gde tvoya damashnyaya rabota?

Don't be late to class! . . . . Ne apazdyvay na urok!

Please study tonight. . . . . Pazhaluysta, pazanimaysya vecherom.

What test are you taking? . . . . Kakoy test ty sdayosh?

Do you need help? . . . . Tebe nuzhna pomosch?

May I help you? . . . . Ya magu tebe pamoch?

Please pay attention. . . . . Pazhaluysta, obratite vnimaniye.

Good work! . . . . Kharoshaya rabota!

Do you understand the test? . . . . Ty panimayesh test?

Do you understand your homework? . . . . Ty panimayesh svayo damashneye zadaniye?

I am proud of you. . . . . Ya gorzhus toboy.

Keep up the good work. . . . . Pradalzhay kharasho rabotat.

Do you know where your next class is? . . . . Ty znayesh gde tvoy sleduyuschiy urok?

How was art class? . . . . Kak prashol urok iskustva?

How was gym class? . . . . Kak prashol urok fizkultury?

How was music class? . . . . Kak prashol urok muzyki?

Quiet please. . . . . Tishe, pazhaluysta.

Please don't interrupt. . . . . Pazhaluysta, ne perebivayte.

You need to write a dscriptive essay. . . . . Vam nuzhno napisat sachineniye.

The homework is due _____. . . . . Tebe nado zdat domashnyuyu raboty do _____.

The test is _____ . . . . Kontro naya rebota budet _____.

Your project is due _____ . . . . Vam nujno zdat vash proekt do _____.

There is no school tomorrow. . . . . Zavtra netu shkoli.

Happy Birthday! . . . . S dnyom razhdeniya!

Where are you going? . . . . Kuda vi edete?

Where do you live? . . . . Gde vi jivete?

Common words and phrases

Hello . . . . Zdravstvuyte.

Goodbye . . . . Do svidaniya.

Please . . . . Pajaluysta.

Excuse me . . . . Izvinite.

Thank you . . . . Spasibo.

You're welcome . . . . Pajaluysta.

Nice to meet you. . . . . Ochen priyatno.

Good morning . . . . Dobroe utro.

Good afternoon . . . . Dobriy den.

Good evening . . . . Dobriy vecher .

Good night . . . . Spokoynoy nochi.

Yes . . . . da

No . . . . net

Maybe . . . . Mojit bit

Open . . . . otkryto
Closed . . . . zakryto
All . . . . vse
A little . . . . nemnogo, malo
A lot . . . . mnogo
Good . . . . horosho
Bad . . . . ploho

Questions
Who? . . . . Jto?
What? . . . . Shto?
Where? . . . . Gdye?
When? . . . . Kagda?
Why? . . . . Pachimu?
How? . . . . Kak?
How much? . . . . Skol'ka?
Where is _____? . . . . Gde _____?
What is this? . . . . Chto eto takoye?
I do not understand.. . . . . Ya ne ponimayu
How do you say this in English? . . . . . . Kak eto skazat po Angliysky?
Do you speak English? . . . . Vy govorite po Angliysky?
What is your name? . . . . Kak vas zovut?
How are you? . . . . Kak dela?
How much does this cost? . . . . Skolko eto stoit?
I will buy it . . . . Ya kuplyu eto.
I would like to buy _____ . . . . Ya hotel by kupit _____.
Do you have _____? . . . . U vas est...?
Do you accept credit cards? . . . . Vy prynymaete kreditnye kartochky?
What time is it? . . . . Kotoryi chas?

Where
Where's the bathroom? . . . . Gde zdes tualet?
Where is _____? . . . . Gde _____?
Airport . . . . aeroport
Train station . . . . vokzal
Bus station . . . . avtovokzal
Subway station . . . . stantsiya metro
Car rental agency . . . . prokat automobiley
Hotel . . . . gostinitsa, otel
Post office . . . . pochta
Bank . . . . bank
Police station . . . . militsiya
Hospital . . . . bolnitsa
Drug store/Pharmacy . . . . apteka
Grocery store, Store . . . . magazin
Restaurant . . . . restoran

School .... shkola
Church .... czerkov
Restrooms .... tualet
Left .... nalevo
Right .... napravo
Far .... daliko
Near .... blizko

Who
Mother .... mat
Father .... otets
Brother .... brat
Sister .... sis'tya
Family .... sim'ya
Husband .... muzh
Wife .... zhena
Son .... syn
Daughter .... doch
Friend .... drug
Teacher .... pripada vatel'
Student .... studyent
Doctor .... vrach
Policeman .... militsiya
Waiter .... afitsiant
I .... ya
We .... mi
You (singular) .... ti, vi
You (plural) vi
They .... oni

What
Train .... poezd
Bus .... avtobus
Room .... komnata
Reservation .... zakaz
Passport .... passport
Ticket .... bilet
Map .... karta
Tourist information .... turisticheskoe byuro
Postcard .... otkrytka
Stamps .... marki
May I see the menu? .... minyu, pazhalusta
I would like to order. .... Ya hotel bi sdelat zakaz.
Please bring the check. ...... pozhaluysta, prinesite shchet.
Breakfast .... zavtrak
Lunch .... obed

Dinner . . . . uzhin
Coffee . . . . kofe
Tea . . . . chay
Milk . . . . malako
Juice . . . . sok
Water . . . . voda
Bread . . . . hleb
Fruit . . . . frukty
Salad . . . . salat
Beef . . . . govyadina
Pork . . . . svinina
Fish . . . . ryba
Chicken . . . . kuritsa
Vegetable . . . . ovoshchi
Dessert . . . . dessert
Salt . . . . sol
Pepper . . . . perets
Beer . . . . pivo
Wine . . . . vino

When

Today . . . . sevodnya
Yesterday . . . . vchera
Tomorrow . . . . zavtra
Now . . . . seychas
Minute . . . . minuta
Hour . . . . chas
Arrive . . . . pribyvat'
Depart . . . . atpra vlyatsya

Day . . . . den
Week . . . . nedelya
Month . . . . mesyats
Year . . . . god

Monday . . . . ponedelnik
Tuesday . . . . vtornik
Wednesday . . . . sreda
Thursday . . . . chetverg
Friday . . . . pyatnitsa
Saturday . . . . subbota
Sunday . . . . voskresenie

January . . . . yanvar
February . . . . fevral
March . . . . mart
April . . . . aprel

May . . . . may
June . . . . iyun
July . . . . iyul
August . . . . avgust
September . . . . sentyabr
October . . . . oktyabr
November . . . . noyabr
December . . . . dekabr

Fall . . . . osen
Winter . . . . zima
Spring . . . . vesna
Summer . . . . leto

How many

zero . . . . nol
one . . . . odin
two . . . . dva
three . . . . tri
four . . . . chetire
five . . . . pyat
six . . . . shest
seven . . . . sem
eight . . . . vosem
nine . . . . devyat
ten . . . . desyat

eleven . . . . odinnadsat
twelve . . . . dvenadsat
thirteen . . . . trinadsat
fourteen . . . . chetyrnadsat
fifteen . . . . pyatnadsat
sixteen . . . . shestnadsat
seventeen . . . . semnadsat
eighteen . . . . vosemnadsat
nineteen . . . . devyatnadsat
twenty . . . . dvadsat

twenty one . . . . dvadsat odin
thirty . . . . tridsat
forty . . . . sorok
fifty . . . . pyatdesyat
sixty . . . . shestdesyat
seventy . . . . semdesyat
eighty . . . . vosemdesyat
ninety . . . . devyanosto
one hundred . . . . sto

Somali

In ancient times, Somalia was known as the biblical and Egyptian land of Punt. Somali is spoken by approximately 8 million people in Somalia, Djibouti, Kenya and Ethiopia. Somalia adopted the Latin (western) alphabet in 1972. Because of the civil war and diaspora, it is estimated that between 15 million to 25 million speakers in the Middle East, Europe, North America and Australia.

Grammar
Somali divides up their nouns and verbs according to the gender with a flexible word owrder

Vowels
The Somali vowels are like English a, e, i, o, u, but different vowel lengths give different meanings to a word.

Consonants and pronunciation

c	a vowel modifier and sounds like the 'h' sound when hissed.
dh	like a flapped 'd' or 'r' by placing the tongue on the roof of the mouth.
kh	is a hard 'ch' as in Bach or loch or lock.
q	is pronounced as 'k' starting at the back of the throat
x	exhaled sound.
'	a pause or stop.

Phrases for school

How are you? . . . . Sidee tahay?

Did you finish your homework? . . . . Madhamay say layligaagii?

What tests do you have today? . . . . Imtixa ukee baadleeday maanta?

Welcome. . . . . Soo dhawoow.

Nice to meet you. . . . . Kulan wanaag san.

Welcome to our school. . . . . Ku soo dhawoowis kuulkeena.

My name is _____. . . . . Magacay gu waa _____.

What is your name? . . . . Magocaa?

Do you understand the teacher? . . . . Mafahamtay macalinka?

You need to turn in your homework everyday. . . . . . Waa inaadiisoo dhiibtaa—layligaaga maalin walba.

Where are you from?. . . . . Xaagee katimid?

Do you have any brothers or sisters? . . . . Ma hay sataa waalo gabdho iyo wiilal?

How are you adjusting to our school?. . . . . Sidee ula gab sanay saa ougsiga?

Do you speak English? . . . . Englishkq maku hadashaa?

Do you play any sports?. . . . . Ciyaaraha ma dhee shaa?

Do you have a girlfriend/boyfriend? . . . . Ma hay sataa saxiib wiilama/gabar?

What is your favorite subject in school? . . . . Waa maxay maadada aad ge ceshahay dugsiga?

What is your worst subject in school? . . . . Waa maxay maadada aad ugunecab tahay Dugsiga?

Where is your homework?. . . . . Aaway layligaagii?

Don't be late to class!. . . . . Ha soo daahiu fasalka!

Please study tonight. . . . . Fadlan caawa soo baro.

What test are you taking?. . . . . Imtixaankee baad gaadanay saa?

Do you need help?. . . . . Wax caawimaad ah miyaad u baahautay?

May I help you? . . . . Maku caawink araa?

Please pay attention. . . . . Fadlan is jir.

Good work!. . . . . Shago Wanaag san!

Do you understand the test? . . . . Ma fahamtay imtixaauka?

Do you understand your homework? . . . . Mafahamty layligaaga?

I am proud of you. . . . . Waa kugufaanaa.

Keep up the good work. . . . . Si Fiican u shaqee.

How was art class? . . . . Sidee buu ahaa fasalkaagii farbarashada?

How was gym class?. . . . . Sidee buul ahaa fasalkaaga jimicsiga?

How was music class?. . . . . Sidee buu ahaa fasalkaaga fanka?

Quiet please. . . . . Fadlan aamus.

Please don't interrupt. . . . . Fadlan hana dhibin.

The homework is due _____. . . . . Homeworka barilgaraba _____.

The test is _____ . . . . Itahan baliyga raba _____.

Your project is due _____. . . . . Project baliyga raba _____.

Your paper is due _____. . . . . Warkadadada balacaraba _____.

There is no school tomorrow. . . . . School barey ma cherto.

Happy Birthday! . . . . Maalintaad dhalatay farxad leh!

Common words and phrases

Hello . . . . Hayye! Or Nabad!

Goodbye . . . . Nabad gelyo!

Please . . . . wan co bar yay ya

Excuse me . . . . Ebana

Thank you . . . . mahadsanid ath

You're Welcome . . . . do fseoe

Good morning . . . . Subax wanaagsan!

Good afternoon . . . . Balab wanaagsan! Galab wanaagsan!

Good evening . . . . Caweys wanaagsan!

Good night . . . . Habeen wanaagsan!

Yes . . . . haa

No . . . . maya, may

Open . . . . fur
Closed . . . . xidhan
Good . . . . wanaagsan
Bad . . . . aeb oononyahiy

Questions

Who? . . . . kuma? or yaa?
What? . . . . maxaa?
When? . . . . goorma?
Where? . . . . xaggee?
Why? . . . . waayo?
How? . . . . sidee?
How much? . . . . waa intee?
Where is _____? . . . . mee? Or meeye?
What is that? . . . . waa maxay kaasi?
I do not understand . . . . Maa fahmo
How do you say this in English? . . . . Sidee Af Engriisi...loogu yidhaahdaa?
Do you speak English? . . . . Af ma ku hadli kartaa Ingriisi?
What is your name? . . . . Magacaa?
How are you? . . . . Iska warran?
How much is this? . . . . waa immisa kanu/tanu?
I would like to buy _____ . . . . Waxa aan rabaa inaan soo iibsado _____.
I'll take it. . . . . Waan qaadan doonaa/ qaadanayaa.
Do you accept credit cards? . . . . Kiridit kaadhka ma qaadataa?
What time is it? . . . . Waa immisadii?

Where

Where's the bathroom? Where is the toilet? . . . . Mee baadku?
Where is _____? . . . . Waa xaggee _____?
Airport . . . . garoonka diyaaradaha/gegida diyaaradaha
Train station . . . . maxaddadda tareenka; isteeshinka tareenka
Bus station . . . . isteeshinka baska
Hotel . . . . huteel
Post office . . . . xafiiska boostadu
Bank . . . . baanku/bangigu
Police station . . . . .booliisku
Hospital . . . . casbitaal
Drug store/Pharmacy . . . . farmasii
Grocery store/store . . . . dukaan
Restaurant . . . . maqaahi; hudheel
School . . . . dugsi; iskuul
Church . . . . kiniisaddu
Restrooms . . . . tooyladku; baytalmaygu

Left . . . . naLYEva
Right . . . . SPRava
Far . . . . fog (ka)
Near . . . . BLISka

Who

Mother . . . . hooyo
Father . . . . aabbe
Brother . . . . aboowe; walaal
Sister . . . . walaal
Family . . . . bah; qoys; extended reer
Husband . . . . ninkayga
Wife . . . . naagtayda
Husband . . . . ninkayga
Son . . . . inan; wiil
Daughter . . . . inan; gabadh
Friend . . . . saaxiibad (F), saaxiib (M)
Teacher . . . . macallin
Student . . . . arday
Doctor . . . . dhaktar
I . . . . Aniga
We . . . . innaga
You (plural) . . . . idinka
They . . . . iyaga

What

Train . . . . tareenka
Bus . . . . gaadiidka; bas
Room . . . . nafar ah
Passport . . . . NacnopT
Ticket . . . . iibsan karaa
Map . . . . PLAN
Tourist information . . . . turiSTIchiski infarMAtiya
Postcard . . . . booskaadh
Stamps . . . . boolo
Can I see the menu please? . . . . Fadlan menyuuga i sii?
I would like to order now. . . . . . Imminka ayaan wax
I would like the bill. . . . . Waxaan rabaa xisaabta
Breakfast . . . . quraac
Lunch . . . . qado
Dinner . . . . casho
Coffee . . . . bun; kaafi
Tea . . . . shaah

Milk . . . . caano
Juice . . . . casiir
Mineral water . . . . biyo macdanaysan
Bread . . . . roodhi
Fruit . . . . midho
Salad . . . . saladh
Beef . . . . hilib lo'aad
Pork . . . . doofaar
Fish . . . . kalluun
Chicken . . . . digaag
Vegetable . . . . khudaar
Dessert . . . . macmacaan
Salt . . . . cusbo
Pepper . . . . basbaas
Wine . . . . waayn

When
Today . . . . maanta
Yesterday . . . . shalay
Tomorrow . . . . berrito
Now . . . . imminka
Minute . . . . daqiiqad
Hour . . . . saacad
Arrive . . . . gaadhcx
Depart . . . . duulid

Day . . . . Dyen'
Week . . . . Nidyelya
Month . . . . Myesits
Year . . . . Got

Monday . . . . Isniin
Tuesday . . . . Salaasa
Wednesday . . . . Arbaca
Thursday . . . . Khamiis
Friday . . . . Jimce
Saturday . . . . Sabti
Sunday . . . . Axad

January . . . . Jeenawery; Janaayo
February . . . . Feebarwery; Febraayo
March . . . . Maarij; Maarso
April . . . . Abriil
May . . . . Meey; Maajo
June . . . . Juun

July . . . . Juulaay; Luulyo
August . . . . Ogos; Agoosto
September . . . . Sibtambar; Sebtember
October . . . . Oktoobar
November . . . . Noofembar
December . . . . Diisembar

Fall . . . . Dayr
Winter . . . . Jiilaal
Spring . . . . Gu'
Summer. . . . . Xagaa

How many
zero . . . . eber
one . . . . kow
two . . . . laba
three . . . . saddex
four . . . . afar
five . . . . shan
six lix
seven . . . . toddoba
eight . . . . siddeed
nine . . . . sagaal
ten . . . . toban

eleven . . . . low iyo toban;
                                koob iyo toban
twelve . . . . laba iyo toban
thirteen . . . . saddex iyo toban
fourteen . . . . afar iyo toban
fifeteen . . . . shan iyo toban
sixteen . . . . lix iyo toban
seventeen . . . . toddoba iyo toban
eighteen . . . . siddeed iyo toban
nineteen . . . . sagaal iyo toban
twenty . . . . labaatan

twenty one . . . . labaatan kow
thirty . . . . soddon
forty . . . . afartan
fifty . . . . konton
sixty . . . . lixdan
seventy . . . . toddobaatan
eighty . . . . siddeetan
ninety . . . . sagaashan
one hundred . . . . boqol

Spanish

Spanish is the official language of Spain, Mexico, Puerto Rico, the Philippines, and every country in Central and South America except Brazil. Spanish is the most popular second language of many people living in the United States. There are over 400 million speakers worldwide.

In Spanish every letter is pronounced except h and occasionally u.

Vowels

Spanish vowels are short and distinct.

a	pronounced 'u' as in luster.
e	pronounced like 'e' as in Elaine.
i	pronounced like 'i' in machine.
o	pronounced like 'o' in hot, spot or lot.
u	pronounced like 'oo' in balloon.

Consonants

The majority of spanish consonants are pronounced like English except for b and v.

c, qu, z - ca, co, cu, que, qui
c and qu are pronounced like the English 'k' and the 'u' is silent in such words as quiero or que.

ce, ci, za, zo, zu
c and z are pronounced like 'th' in think.

g, gu - ga, go, gu, gue, gui
pronounced like 'g' in garbage.

g, i - ge, gi, ja, je, ii, jo, iu
g and j are pronounced as Scottish 'ch' in loch.

y
pronounced like 'i' in hoy or soy and at the beginning of a syllable 'y' is pronounced like a soft 'j' in mayor.

r, rr - r
between vowels, r is slightly rolled. At the beginning of a word, 'r' is rolled more strongly. 'rr' is always rolled strongly.

ll   like 'lli' in million.

ñ   as 'ni' in onion and España .

h   h 'is' silent in Spanish

Note that ch, ll, ñ, and rr are considered single letters in Spanish and are, therefore listed after, c, l, n and r in dictionaries. The final -d (e.g. usted, Madrid) is usually dropped.

Phrases for school

How are you?	Como esta?
Did you finish your homework?	Termino usted sus deberes?
What tests do you have today?	Que examenes tiene usted hoy?
Welcome.	Bienvenida.
Nice to meet you.	Agradable reunirlo.
Welcome to our school.	Bienvenida a nuestra escuela.
My name is _____.	Mi nombre es _____. or Me llamo _____.
What is your name?	Como se llama?
Do you understand the teacher?	Entiende usted al maestro?
You need to turn in your homework everyday.	Usted necesita entregar sus tareas diarios.
Do you have any questions?	Tiene usted cualquiera pregunta?
Where are you from?	De donde son eres?
Do you have any brothers or sisters?	Tiene usted hermano o hermonas?
How are you adjusting to our school?	Como sean usted ajuste a nuestra escuela?
Do you speak English?	Habla usted ingles? Or Tu hables ingles?
Do you play any sports?	Juega usted deportes?
Do you have a girlfriend/boyfriend?	Tiene usted a una amiga/amigo?
What is your favorite subject in school?	Que es su sujeto favorito en la escuela?
What is your worst subject in school?	Que es su sujeto peor en la escuela?
Where is your homework?	Donde estan sus deberes?
Don't be late to class!	No sea tarde a la clase!
Please study tonight.	Por favor estudio esta noche.
What test are you taking?	Que prueba toma usted?
Do you need help?	Necesita usted ayuda?
May I help you?	Lo puedo ayudar yo?
Please pay attention.	Preste atencion por favor.
Good work!	Bueno trabajo!
Do you understand the test?	Entiende usted la prueba?
Do you understand your homework?	Entiende usted sus deberes?
I am proud of you.	Soy orgulloso de usted.
Keep up the good work.	Mantengase al ritmo del trabajo bueno.
Do you know where your next class is?	Sabe usted donde usted proxima clase es?
How was art class?	Como es la clase de arte?
How was gym class?	Como es la clase de gimnasio?
How was music class?	Como es la clase de musica?
Quiet please.	La calma por favor.
Please don't interrupt.	Por favor no interrumpa.

You need to write a descriptive paper. . . . . Usted necesita escribir un papel descriptivo.

You need to write a narrative paper. . . . . Usted necesita escribir un papel narrativo.

You need to write a comparison/contrast paper. . . . . . . Usted necesita escribir una comparacion.
papel de contraste.

You need to write a poem. . . . . Usted necesita escribir un poema.

The homework is due _____ . . . . Los deberes son debidos _____.

The test is _____ . . . . La prueba es _____.

Your project is due _____. . . . . Su proyecto es debido _____.

Your paper is due _____ . . . . Su papel es debido _____.

There is no school tomorrow. . . . . No hay escuela manana.

Happy Birthday! . . . . Feliz cumpleanos!

Where are you going? . . . . Hacia dónde vas?

Where do you live? . . . . Dónde vive usted?

Common words and phrases

Hello. . . . . Hola.

Goodbye . . . . Adiós.

Please. . . . . Por favor.

Excuse me. . . . . Perdoname.

Thank you. . . . . Gracias.

You're welcome. . . . . De nada.

Nice to meet you. . . . . Encantado de conocerle.

Good morning. . . . . Buenos días.

Good afternoon. . . . . Buenas tardes.

Good evening. . . . . Buenas noches.

Good night. . . . . Buenas noches.

Yes . . . . sí

No . . . . no

Maybe . . . . quizás

Open . . . . abierto

Closed . . . . cerrado

All . . . . todo

A little . . . . un poco

A lot . . . . mucho

Good . . . . bueno

Bad . . . . mal

Questions

Who? . . . . Quién?

What? . . . . Qué?

When? . . . . Cuando?

Where? . . . . Donde?

Why? . . . . Por qué?

How?. . . . . Como?

How much? . . . . Cuanto?

Where is _____? . . . . Donde está?

What is this? . . . . Que es?

I do not understand. . . . . No entiendo

How do you say this in English? . . . . . . Cómo se dice esto en Inglés

Do you speak English? . . . . Habla usted Inglés?

What is your name? . . . . Como se llama usted? Cual es su nombre?

How are you? . . . . Como estas? Que pasa?

How much does this cost? . . . . Cuanto cuesta? Cual es el precio?

I will buy it. . . . . Lo compro.

I would like to buy _____ . . . . Me gustaria comprar _____.

Do you have _____?. . . . . Tiene usted _____ ?

Do you accept credit cards? . . . . Aceptan tarjetas de credito?

What time is it? . . . . Qué hora es?

Where

Where's the bathroom? . . . . Donde está el baño?

Where is _____? . . . . Donde esta _____?

Airport . . . . el aeropuerto

Train station . . . . la estación del metro

Bus station . . . . la estación de autobuses

Subway station . . . . la estación del metro

Car rental agency . . . . agencia de alquiler de coches; Un alquilador automovil

Hotel . . . . el hotel

Post office . . . . la oficina de correo

Bank . . . . el banco

Police station . . . . la estacion de policia; la comisaria de policia

Hospital . . . . el hospital

Pharmacy . . . . la farmacia

Store . . . . la tienda

Restaurant . . . . el restaurante

School . . . . la escuela

Church . . . . la iglesia

Restrooms . . . . los banos, los sanitarios, los servicios

Left . . . . la izquierda

Right . . . . derecho

Far . . . . lejos

Near . . . . cercano

Who

Mother . . . . la madre

Father . . . . el padre

Brother . . . . el hermano

Sister . . . . la hermana

Family . . . . la familia

Wife . . . . la esposa

Son . . . . el hijo
Friend . . . . el amigo (M), la amiga (F)
Teacher . . . . el maestro
Student . . . . el estudiante
Doctor . . . . el médico
Policeman . . . . la policía
Waiter . . . . el camarero

I . . . . yo
We . . . . nosotros
You (singular) . . . . tú (informal)
You (singular) . . . . usted (formal)
You (plural) . . . . ustedes (vosotros)
They . . . . ellos (M), ellas (F)

What
Train . . . . el tren
Bus . . . . el autobus
Room . . . . el cuarto
Reservation . . . . la reservación
Passport . . . . el pasaporte
Ticket . . . . el boleto, el billete
Map . . . . la mapa
Tourist information . . . . información de turísta
Postcard . . . . la tarjeta postal
Stamps . . . . los sellos, los timbres, las estampillas
May I see a menu, please? . . . . . Puedo ver yo un menu, por favor?
I would like to order. . . . . Apreciaría ordenar.
Please bring the check. . . . . Me trae la cuenta por favor?
Breakfast . . . . el desayuno
Lunch . . . . el almuerzo (la comida)
Dinner . . . . la cena
Beverage . . . . la bebida
Coffee . . . . el café
Milk . . . . la leche
Tea . . . . el té
Juice . . . . el jugo, el zumo
Water . . . . el agua
Wine . . . . el vino
Bread . . . . el pan
Beef . . . . la ternera, la carne de vaca, el res
Pork . . . . el puerco
Fish . . . . el pescado
Chicken . . . . el pollo
Vegetable . . . . las verduras
Fruit . . . . la fruta

Salad . . . . la ensalada
Dessert . . . . el postre
Salt . . . . la sal
Pepper . . . . la pimienta

When
Today . . . . hoy
Yesterday . . . . ayer
Tomorrow . . . . mañana
Now . . . . ahora
Minute . . . . minuto
Hour . . . . hora
Arrive . . . . llega
Depart . . . . parte

Day . . . . el día
Week . . . . la semana
Month . . . . el mes
Year . . . . el año

Monday . . . . lunes
Tuesday . . . . martes
Wednesday . . . . miércoles
Thursday . . . . jueves
Friday . . . . viernes
Saturday . . . . sábado
Sunday . . . . domingo

January . . . . enero
February . . . . febrero
March . . . . marzo
April . . . . abril
May . . . . mayo
June . . . . junio
July . . . . julio
August . . . . agosto
September . . . . septiembre
October . . . . octubre
November . . . . noviembre
December . . . . diciembre

Fall . . . . el otoño
Winter . . . . el invierno
Spring . . . . la primavera
Summer . . . . el verano

How many
zero . . . . cero
one . . . . uno
two . . . . dos
three . . . . tres
four . . . . cuatro
five . . . . cinco
six . . . . seis
seven . . . . siete
eight . . . . ocho
nine . . . . nueve
ten . . . . diez

eleven . . . . once
twelve . . . . doce
thirteen . . . . trece
fourteen . . . . catorce
fifteen . . . . quince
sixteen . . . . dieciséis
seventeen . . . . diecisiete
eighteen . . . . dieciocho
nineteen . . . . diecinueve
twenty . . . . veinte

twenty one . . . . veintiuno, veinte y uno
thirty . . . . treinta
forty . . . . cuarenta
fifty . . . . cincuenta
sixty . . . . sesenta
seventy . . . . setenta
eighty . . . . ochenta
ninety . . . . noventa
one hundred . . . . cien

Swahili

Swahili is the most widely spoken African language in East Africa and the Congo region as a governmental and trade language. Many Swahili speakers have their local tongues as a native language and use Swahili to speak with outsiders. Swahili is a Bantu language, but it also has words from Arabic due to Islamic influence.

Pronunciation

Vowels

There are five vowel sounds that are short and have dipthongs with some Italian and Spanish values.

Swahili	English Sound
a	'ah'
e	'bay '
i	'see'
o	'low'
u	'too'

Consonants

Consonants in Swahili generally have English values, but as in the case of vowels, there are considerable differences.

p, t and **k**	voiced, stops, and is pronounced as you suck air into the mouth and then exhaled.
b, d and **g**	voiced stops are pronounced as air is sucked into the mouth as they are released, and the 'g' is also hard like in guard and goat.
f, v, s and **z**	pronounced the same in English, and 's' is never pronounced as an English 'z'.
m and **n**	pronounced the same in English and sometimes before other consonants.
ny	pronounced a the n in manana (spanish for word tomorrow), and the in ni in the word onion.
ng	pronounced as the 'ng' in ding.

ch	sounds as a soft 'ch' as in cheek, church.
j	as in the word job.
w, y and h r	Swahili h may be written as 'kh' which symbolizes a sound similar to hard 'ch'. 'r' is different from the English r; it is similar to the Spanish tapped 'r' as in pero (but).
l	as in English when in beginning position, e.g. leak; second language speakers tend not to distinguish 'r' and 'l''.
th	as in think or thin
dh	as in that or then
gh	pronounced as a hard 'g' in garage.
sh	as in brush.

Phrases for school

How are you?	Jambo?
Did you finish your homework?	Umemaliza durusi yako?
What tests do you have today?	Una mtihani upi leo?
Welcome.	Karibu.
Nice to meet you.	Vizuri kujuana.
Welcome to our school.	Karibu kwa shule yetu.
My name is _____.	Jina langu ni _____.
What is your name?	Jina lako nani?
Do you understand the teacher?	Unamuelewa Mwalimu?
You need to turn in your homework everyday.	Unatakikana urudishe durusi yako kila siku.
Where are you from?	Unatoka wapi?
Do you have any brothers or sisters?	Una ndugu yeyote/dada au kaka?
How are you adjusting to our school?	Unapenda vipi shule yetu?
Do you speak English?	Unazungumza kiengereza?
Do you play any sports?	Unacheza mchezo yeyote?
Do you have a girlfriend/boyfriend?	Una ratiki wa kike/mume?
What is your favorite subject in school?	Unaipenda usomo gani shuleni?
What is your worst subject in school?	Somo gani huipendi shulem.
Where is your homework?	Iko wapi udurusi yako?
Don't be late to class!	Usichelewe darasani!
Please study tonight.	Tafadhali soma usiko.
What test are you taking?	Unachukua mtihani upi?
Do you need help?	Unataka msaidizi?

May I help you? . . . . Unkependa nikusaidie?

Please pay attention. . . . . Tafadhali sikiliza kwa makini.

Good work! . . . . Kazi nzuri!

Do you understand the test? . . . . Unaelewa mitihani?

Do you understand your homework? . . . . Unaelewa durusa nyumbani lako ya?

I am proud of you. . . . . Nimekufuha ia Kwa wewe.

Keep up the good work. Endelea kazi yako nzuri.

Do you know where your next class is? . . . . Unaijua darasa lako lengine?

How was art class? . . . . Ulikua vipi darasa la michoro?

How was gym class? . . . . Ulikua vipi riadha?

How was music class? . . . . Ulikua vipi darasa la musiki?

Quiet please. . . . . Nyamaza tafadhali.

Please don't interrupt. . . . . Tafadhli usisumbue.

The homework is due _____. . . . . Darasa ya nybani nyumbani _____.

Happy Birthday! . . . . Hongera!

Where are you going? . . . . Unakwenda wapi?

Where do you live? . . . . Unaishi wapi?

Common words and phrases

Hello. . . . . Jambo, Hujambo

Goodbye. . . . . Kwa heri (to one), Kwa herini (to many)

Please. . . . . Tafadhali

Excuse me. . . . . Kunradhi

Thank you. . . . . Asante

You're welcome. . . . . Starehe

Nice to meet you. . . . . Nafurahi kukuona

Good morning. . . . . Habari za asubuhi?

Good afternoon. . . . . Habari za mchana?

Good evening. . . . . Habari za jioni?

Good night. . . . . Habari za usiku?

Yes . . . . ndiyo

No . . . . hapana

Maybe . . . . labda

Open . . . . imefunguliwa, Wazi

Closed . . . . imefungwa

All . . . . yote

A little . . . . kidogo

A lot . . . . nyingi

Good . . . . njema, nzuri, salama

Bad . . . . mbaya

Questions

Who? . . . . nani?

What? . . . . nini?

When? . . . . lini?

Where? .... Wapi?

How? .... Kama?

How much? .... Kama ingi?

Where is ____? .... Iko wapi ____?

What is this? .... Hii ni nini?

I do not understand. .... Sifahamu

How do you say this in English? .... Unasemaje kiswahili kwa Kiingereza?

Do you speak ____? .... Unaweza kusema Kiingereza ____?

What is your name? .... Jina lako nani? Wewe nani?

How are you? .... Habari gani? Uhali gani?

How much does this cost? .... Hii ni bei gani?

I will buy it............................. Nitainunua.

I would like to buy ____ .... Ninataka kununua ____.

Do you have ____? .... Unayo ____?

Do you accept credit cards? .... Naweza kutumia kadi ya benki?

What time is it? .... Ni saa ngapi sasa?

Where

Where's the bathroom? Where is the toilet? .... Choo kiko wapi?

Where is ____? .... iko wapi ____?

Airport .... kiwanja cha ndege

Train station .... stesheni ya gari la moshi

Bus station .... stesheni ya basi

Car rental agency .... pahali pa kukomboa gari za kibinafs

Hotel .... hoteli

Post office .... nyumba ya posta

Bank .... benki

Police station .... kwa ofisi ya polisi

Hospital .... hosptali

Pharmacy .... duka la madawa

Grocery store, store .... akiba

Restaurant .... mkahawa

School .... chuo, shule

Church .... kanisa

Restrooms .... iko wapi nyumba ya kuogea, Choo

Left .... kushoto

Right .... kulia

Near .... karibu

Who

Father .... Baba

Mother .... Mama

Brother .... kaka, ndugu

Sister .... dada

Family .... ndugu

Husband . . . . mume
Wife . . . . mke
Son . . . . mwana
Daughter . . . . binti
Friend . . . . rafiki
Teacher . . . . mwalimu
Doctor . . . . mganga, daktari

I . . . . mimi
We . . . . sisi
You (singular, familiar) . . . . wewe
You (plural) . . . . nyinyi
They . . . . wao

What
Train . . . . gari la moshi
Bus . . . . basi
Room . . . . chumba
Reservation . . . . akiba
Passport . . . . pasi, pasipoti
Ticket . . . . tikiti
Map . . . . ramani
Tourist information . . . . wapi ofisi ya habari
Postcard . . . . kadi ya posta
Stamps . . . . stampu za posta
Please bring the check. . . . . Tafadhali, letee checki.
Breakfast . . . . chakula cha asubuhi
Lunch . . . . chakula cha mchana
Dinner . . . . chakula cha usiku
Coffee . . . . kahawa
Tea . . . . chai
Juice . . . . maji ya matunda
Milk . . . . maziwa
Water . . . . maji
Bread . . . . mkate
Fruit . . . . matunda
Salad . . . . mboga mbichi
Beef . . . . nyama ya ngombe
Pork . . . . nyama ya nguruwe
Fish . . . . samaki
Chicken . . . . kuku
Vegetable . . . . mboga
Dessert . . . . switi, kitindamlo
Salt . . . . chumvi
Pepper . . . . pilipili
Beer . . . . pombe
Wine . . . . divai

When

Today	leo
Yesterday	jana
Tomorrow	kesho
Arrive	kufika
Depart	kuondoka
Day	siku
Week	wiki
Month	mwezi
Year	mwaka

Monday	jumatatu
Tuesday	jumanne
Wednesday	jumatano
Thursday	alhamisi
Friday	ijumaa
Saturday	jumamosi
Sunday	jumapili

January	Januari
February	Februari
March	Machi
April	Aprili
May	Mei
June	Juni
July	Julai
August	Augosti
September	Septemba
October	Oktoba
November	Novemba
December	Disemba

How many

zero	sifuri
one	moja
two	mbili
three	tatu
four	nne
five	tano
six	sita
seven	saba
eight	nane
nine	tisa
ten	kumi

eleven	kumi na moja
twelve	kumi na mbili
thirteen	kumi na tatu
fourteen	kumi na nne
fifteen	kumi na tano
sixteen	kumi na sita
seventeen	kumi na saba
eighteen	kumi na nane
nineteen	kumi na tisa
twenty	ishirini

twenty one	ishirini na moja
thirty	thelathini
forty	arobaini
fifty	hamsini
sixty	sitini
seventy	sabini
eighty	themanini
ninety	tisini
one hundred	mia moja

Vietnamese

Vietnamese is the national language of the Socialist Republic of Vietnam, spoken by over 70 million people. Many refugees fled the nation after the fall of South Vietnam in the 1970's. Significant numbers of Vietnamese speakers exist in the United States and Australia. The language was first translated and compiled into dictionaries by Catholic missionaries in the sixteenth century.

Tones

The Vietnamese language has different sounds. The sounds are short with single consonants with one or more groups of vowels. There are six tones in Vietnamese such as no tone, raising, falling, questioning, falling-raising, and weighing. For example, the word "ma" can have six different meanings depending on the tone.

No tone	ma	ghost
Raising	má	mother
Falling	mà	that
Questioning	mả	tomb
Falling-raising	mã	horse
Weighing	mạ	fur

Vowels

There are many vowels and groups of vowels in the Vietnamese language.

a	as in father	i	as in see
â	long a sound	ia	as in Asia
ă	back, pack, sack	ie	as in yes
ai	as in buy	o	as in door
ao	as in now	oa	as in moi(French)
au	as in Autumn	oa	stack and pack
ay	as in day	oai	bye, why
ây	as in David	oay	as in Uruguay
e	as in Blaire	oe	as in where
ê	as in café	oi	as in choice

o	as in Bordeaux	uy	as u in French
oi	as in toy	uya	as French culture
u	as in hoo	uyen	as in when
ua	as in Ecuador	uyu	as in new
ue	in a question	y	as in see
ui	like oo-ee	ye	as in yen
uôi	as in way-ee	yeu	as in yes

Consonants

Many groups of consonants are pronounced like single consonants.
For example, all consonants not listed below are pronounced like they are in English.

d	as 'z' in zero	ng, ngh	as in nguyen
gh	like 'g' in go	ph	like 'f' as in fur
gi	like 'y' in yes	tr	as in try
kh	like German 'ch' as in ich	v	pronounced as 'y' to
nh	like French 'gn' in champagne		

Phrases for school

How are you?	Bạn có khoẻ không?
Did you finish your homework?	Bạn đã làm bài tập của bạn chưa?
What tests do you have today?	Bạn có bài kiểm tra nào hôm nay?
Welcome.	Chào mừng
Nice to meet you.	Hân hạnh được gặp bạn
Welcome to our school..	Chào mừng bạn vào trường của chúng tôi.
My name is _____	Tên tôi là _____ .
What is your name?	Bạn tên là gì?
Do you understand the teacher?	Bạn có hiểu cô thầy không?
You need to turn in your homework everyday.	Bạn cần phải nộp bài tập của bạn mỗi ngày
Where are you from?	Bạn từ đâu đến?
Do you have any brothers or sisters?	Bạn có anh em không?
Do you speak English?	Bạn có nói tiếng Anh không?
Do you play any sports?	Bạn có chơi thể thao không?
Do you have a girlfriend/boyfriend?	Bạn có bạn gái/trai không?
What is your favorite subject in school?	Bạn thích môn nào nhất?
What is your worst subject in school?	Bạn ghét nhất môn nào?
Where is your homework?	Bài tập của bạn đâu?
Don't be late to class!	Đừng đến lớp trễ.
Please study tonight.	Xin học bài tối nay.
What test are you taking?	Bạn đang làm bài kiểm tra nào?
Do you need help?	Bạn cần giúp đỡ không?

May I help you?	Tôi có thể giúp gì cho bạn?
Please pay attention.	Xin chú ý.
Good work!	Bài tốt (làm tốt)!
Do you understand the test?	Bạn có hiểu bài kiểm tra không?
Do you understand your homework?	Bạn có hiểu bài tập của bạn không?
I am proud of you.	Tôi hãnh diện cho bạn.
Keep up the good work.	Giữ việc làm tốt của bạn
Do you know where your next class is?	Bạn có biết lớp kế tiếp của bạn ở đâu không?
How was art class?	Lớp hoạ như thế nào?
How was gym class?	Lớp thể dục như thế nào?
How was music class?	Lớp nhạc như thế nào?
Quiet please.	Xin giữ im lặng.
Please don't interrupt.	Xin đừng phá rối.
The homework is due _____.	Xin nộp lên bài của bạn_____.
The test is _____	Bài kiểm tra _____.
Happy Birthday!	Chúc mừng sinh nhật!

Common words and phrases

Hello	Xin chào
Goodbye	Tạm biệt
Please	Xin vui lòng
Excuse me	Xin lỗi
Thank you	Cám ơn
You're welcome	Không có chi
Nice to meet you	Rất hân hạnh
Good morning	Xin chào
Good afternoon	Xin chào
Good evening	Xin chào
Good night	Chúc ngủ ngon
Yes	Có/Vâng/Dạ
No	Không
Maybe	Có thể
Open	Mở
Closed	Đóng
All	Tất cả
A little	Ít
A lot	Nhiều
Good	Tốt
Bad	Xấu

Questions

Who?	Ai; người nào?
What?	Nào; gì; cái gì?
Where?	Ở đâu?
When?	Khi; lúc; trong khi mà?
Why?	Tại sao?
How?	Thế nào?

Where is _____ ? .... Ở đâu _____ ?

What is this? .... Cái gì đây?

I do not understand. .... Tôi không hiểu.

How do you say this in English? .... Cái này tiếng Anh nói thế nào?

Do you speak English? .... Anh(m)/Chị(f) có nói tiếng Anh không?

What is your name? .... Bạn tên là gì?

How are you? .... Bạn có khoẻ không?

What is your name? .... Bạn tên là gì?

How much does this cost? .... Cái này giá bao nhiêu?

What is this? .... Cái này là cái gì?

I will buy it. .... Tôi sẽ mua cái này.

I would like to buy _____. .... Tôi muốn mua _____.

Do you have _____? .... Bạn có _____ không?

Do you accept credit cards? .... Bạn có nhận thẻ tín dụng không?

What time is it? .... Mấy giờ rồi?

Where

Where's the bathroom? Where is the toilet? .... Nhà vệ sinh ở đâu?

Where is _____? .... Ở đâu _____?

Airport .... Sân bay

Train station .... Ga xe lửa

Bus station .... Bến xe buýt

Subway station .... Bến tàu điện ngầm

Car rental agency .... Đại lý cho mướn xe

Hotel .... Khách xạn/Hotel

Post office .... Bưu điện

Bank .... Ngân hàng

Police station .... Đồn cảnh sát

Hospital .... Bệnh viện

Pharmacy .... Dược

Grocery store/store .... Cửa hàng

Restaurant .... Nhà hàng

School .... Trường học

Church .... Nhà thờ

Restrooms .... Nhà vệ sinh

Left .... Trái

Right .... Phải

Far .... Xa

Near .... Gần

Who

Father .... Bố/Ba

Mother .... Mẹ/Má

Brother .... Anh/em trai

Sister .... Chị/Em

Family .... Gia đình

Husband .... Chồng

Wife .... Vợ

Son	Con trai
Daughter	Con gái
Friend	Bạn
Teacher	Thầy giáo; gíáo viên
Student	Sinh viên; học sinh
Doctor	Bác sĩ
Policeman	Cảnh sát
Waiter	người hầu bàn
I	Tôi
We	Chúng tôi
You (singular)	Anh (M), Chị (F), Ông (M), Bà (F)
You (plural)	Các ông (M), Các bà (F)
They	Họ

What

Train	Xe lửa
Bus	Xe buýt
Room	Phòng
Reservation	Đặt chỗ trước
Passport	Hộ chiếu
Ticket	Vé
Map	Bản đồ
Tourist information	Hướng dẫn du lịch
Postcard	Bưu ảnh
Stamps	Tem
May we see the menu?	Chúng tôi có thể xem thực đơn không?
Please bring the check	Tôi muốn trả tiền
Breakfast	Ăn sáng
Lunch	Ăn trưa
Dinner	Ăn tối
Coffee	Cafe
Tea	Trà
Milk	Sữa
Juice	Nước trái cây
Water	Nước
Bread	Bánh mì
Fruit	Trái cây
Salad	Salat, gỏi
Beef	Thịt bò
Pork	Thịt heo
Fish	Cá
Chicken	Thịt gà
Vegetable	Rău
Dessert	Tráng miệng
Salt	Muối
Pepper	Tiêu

When

Today .... Hôm nay
Yesterday .... Hôm qua
Tomorrow .... Ngày mai
Now .... Hiện tại; lúc này
Minute .... Một phút
Arrive .... Đến
Depart .... Rời

Day .... Ngày
Week .... Tuần
Month .... Tháng
Year .... Năm

Monday .... Thứ Hai
Tuesday .... Thứ Ba
Wednesday .... Thứ Tư
Thursday .... Thứ Năm
Friday .... Thứ Sáu
Saturday .... Thứ Bảy
Sunday .... Chủ Nhật

January .... Tháng Một/Giêng
February .... Tháng Hai
March .... Tháng Ba
April .... Tháng Tư
May .... Tháng Năm
June .... Tháng Sáu
July .... Tháng Bảy
August .... Tháng Tám
September .... Tháng Chín
October .... Tháng Mười
November .... Tháng Mười Một
December .... Tháng Mười Hai

Fall .... Mùa Thu
Winter .... Mùa Đông
Spring .... Mùa Xuân
Summer .... Mùa Hè/Hạ

How many

zero .... không
one .... một
two .... hai
three .... ba
four .... bốn
five .... năm
six .... sáu
seven .... bảy
eight .... tám
nine .... chín
ten .... mười

eleven .... mười một
twelve .... mười hai
thirteen .... mười ba
fourteen .... mười bốn
fifteen .... mười lăm
sixteen .... mười sáu
seventeen .... mười bảy
eighteen .... mười tám
nineteen .... mười chín
twenty .... hai mươi

twenty one .... hai mươi mốt
thirty .... ba mươi
forty .... bốn mươi
fifty .... năm mươi
sixty .... sáu mươi
seventy .... bảy mươi
eighty .... tám mươi
ninety .... chín mươi
one hundred .... một trăm